SOMERSET WILD FLOWERS

A GUIDE TO
THEIR IDENTIFICATION

Bernard Storer
with David and Felicity Reid

First published in Great Britain in 2014

Copyright © Bernard Storer 2014

All rights reserved. No part of this publication may be reproduced, stored in a retrieval system, or transmitted in any form or by any means without the prior permission of the copyright holder.

British Library Cataloguing-in-Publication Data A CIP record for this title is available from the British Library

ISBN 978 0 85710 089 4

PiXZ Books
Halsgrove House, Ryelands Business Park,
Bagley Road, Wellington, Somerset TA21 9PZ
Tel: 01823 653777
Fax: 01823 216796
email: sales@halsgrove.com

An imprint of Halstar Ltd, part of the Halsgrove group of companies
Information on all Halsgrove titles is available at: www.halsgrove.com

Printed and bound in China by Everbest Printing Co Ltd

Acknowledgements

Without a great deal of help, we feel that this book could still be in our minds as "one of those things we might do some day".

Foremost of our helpers, we must thank Lynn Stephens of "Lynnz Printz", Weston-zoyland. She has taken in a mixture of badly typed notes, hand written material which is even harder to decipher and a varied collection of photographs. All this she has turned into a readable whole. She has also had patience whilst we have rephrased the text and moved and substituted photographs. Without her help this book would not have seen the light of day.

Secondly we must thank Helen and Edward Wells for their kind permission to use twenty of their photographs. We are especially grateful since their photographs are of plants difficult to find.

We must also thank those plant nurseries who provided us with material (to accepted conservation standards).

Especially we would like to thank British Wildflower Plants of Burlingham Gardens, Norfolk, Naturescape of Langar, Nottinghamshire and Mires Beck Nursery of Brough, Yorkshire.

Back to Somerset, our thanks are due to their Rare Plants Group for their guidance to some of the counties varieties and general help and encouragement.

Finally, we must thank friends who acted as guinea pigs when we wanted to eliminate "botany-speak" and generally encouraged us.

Introduction

It may seem that with so many of our surroundings dominated by man-made structures, there are few places left where wild things can grow. However, our wild plants can be found everywhere. I have seen Treacle Mustard growing in a patch of mud outside a fish and chip shop, the dramatic blue Chicory outside a B&Q, Fringed Water-lily in an old brick pit and the intriguing Lizard Orchid growing on a golf course.

This book is for those people who have a general interest in plants, want to know a bit more about them and want to be able to put a name to them.

Some general knowledge of plants is helpful but not necessary. This book uses pictures to guide the user and tries to avoid the technical terminology of 'academic' books.

The book also points out that identification does not depend solely on the flower. Where, for example, leaf-shape is a guide, then a photograph of the leaf is included.

For the absolute beginners, a simple photographic guide to the small amount of terminology is included.

If recognising them, knowing what these things are, what they are called, encourages the reader to take further interest in wild flowers, to appreciate their beauty and to understand their struggle to survive and not to dismiss them as 'weeds' then that is all to the good.

In 1997, P.R. Green, I.P. Green and C.A. Crouch produced *The Atlas Flora of Somerset*. This amplifies the work done by earlier botanists, particularly Capt R.G.B. Roe whose Flora is the base on which later enthusiasts have built. The *Atlas* describes in detail where the wild plants of Somerset could be found. It is left to the reader to find out how to identify the plants. Depending on their expertise, readers could use either an academic Flora or a slightly less formal pocket guide. However, nearly all these guides rely on written descriptions, even if the book carries many illustrations, and these written guides tend to use specialised terminology. We have tried to avoid this. For readers who have access to the *Atlas* we have included the appropriate page number of the entry in that book. This entry is preceded by the letters A.P. (Atlas Page) and follows after the plant's name. However, we think that it is likely that many readers, who do not have access to the *Atlas*, will come across plants that arouse their curiosity. This book will help them to name the plant.

Using the Book

As children, many of us learned what daisies, dandelions, bluebells, foxgloves etc looked like because we had seen them, or illustrations of them, and our parents or teachers had told us their names.

We certainly did not consult the academic literature of the time and learn to recognise a foxglove by 'the flowers are in a long terminal, one-sided raceme'. What we are aiming to do in this book is to return to the simple, basic way of identifying plants i.e. by seeing what they look like. To this end the photographs are the key guides, the text is there simply to tell the reader exactly what to look for in the photographs.

When identifying plants, some are very easy to name because there are no other plants like them e.g. Foxglove, Ivy, Water-lily and so on.

Other plants may be one of a group of similar relatives but still can be recognised by one feature. Thus Lesser Celandine is one of the group of plants in the Buttercup Family with a cup of yellow petals, but it is the only one of the group to have, usually, 8 petals.

In other cases it may be a combination of two or more characters that help us to put a name to it. The leaf shape distinguishes the Spearworts from the rest of the Buttercup Family, but the individual species of Spearwort can be separated by examining the flowers and the leaves.

We visualise that most people using this book will have seen a plant and want to know what it is called. If they know, or can make a reasonable guess at the plant's Family then they can go straight to that section.

The next step is to read the brief list of the Family's characteristics and check them against the unknown plant. This should confirm that the reader is in the correct section. The reader may be quite satisfied to be able to identify the plants as e.g. a Speedwell. It is then up to the individual to decide whether or not to go forward and try to find out which of the Speedwells is present. This can be done by further reading and especially looking at the photographs of the different species.

The reader now becomes a viewer, looking at the photographs to find a match and using the text only as a guide as to what to look for. Having found the match then the viewer can choose either the English name or the scientific one.

Within the Family, the plants are usually arranged so that those with a unique feature (or features) come first, e.g. Yellow Archangel is the only member of the Dead-nettle Family to have large yellow flowers. With some of the very large Families it is sometimes easier to pick out a small group e.g. the few members of the Dandelion Family which have blue petals.

If the specimen does not correspond to the first photograph, then move on to the second and so on until a match is found.

If the reader/viewer does not know to which Family the plant belongs then it is a case of going through the book until photographs of the appropriate kind appear and then looking more closely. This may not be a scientific method but is very commonly used.

Terminology

After may years of working with and talking and writing about wildlife, we have found that it is unwise to be too positive with any statement. Thus if we write that 'Buttercups are yellow' then the ordinary reader will accept this in the way in which it is meant. However, someone will tell us that they have a buttercup with white petals or they will point out that there are many species in the Buttercup Family and that many of them are not yellow. All this is to explain why terms such as 'usually' or 'normally' are used in the text.

The variability of all living things makes it difficult to be too dogmatic in giving precise features as diagnostics to identification.

One must always bear in mind that the identification and classification of plants and animals is a human activity and the living things themselves play no active part in it. The large striped member of the Cat Family does not care whether we call it a Tiger or a Teasel. In Shakespearean terms 'a rose by any other name would smell as sweet'.

Humans may spend a lot of time in trying to determine the relationship between two groups. But, whatever we decide, it does not mean that the plants are going to start exchanging birthday cards with their new-found relations.

Because classifying and identifying is a human activity, it is like all of them, liable to inaccuracies. This is realised when some new research shows that two plants thought to be 'second cousins' are really 'first cousins'. But the plants themselves, to quote Rhet Butler 'don't give a damn'.

The very term 'wildflower' or 'wild' flower carries uncertainties. We all have a concept of 'wild'; the plant has got to its growing place naturally and has developed without help or hindrance from humans. On the other hand, cultivated plants have been sited by humans and tended by them. Indeed they have possibly been bred, selected and so on before being planted out. But cultivated plants have a habit of escaping, seeds get carried away and so on. The cultivated plant then grows freely; is it now a wild flower?

Some authorities do not accept these escapees as wild plants, especially when they have originated from areas far away and brought here by us. Others take the view that they are here, doing well and should be accepted. We have taken this second view.

Even the word 'flower' can be used ambiguously. We refer to a 'flower-bed' or a bank of 'wildflowers' when we are really referring to the plants. Probably this is because we notice the flowers rather than the leaves etc. This view also applies to grasses. Because they do not have obvious flowers, to some people they 'don't count'. On the other hand some gardens have ferns in the 'flower-bed' - despite the fact that ferns do not bear flowers. Here we have excluded all those plants that do not have flowers but included all those that do, no matter how small or insignificant the flowers may be.

Classification

Botanists divide the Plant Kingdom into a number of smaller groups. These are then subdivided and so on.

The largest of these groups is a Phylum (plural Phyla).

This in turn is split into Classes and Classes into Orders. Orders are then divided into Families.

A Family is a group of plants with the same basic pattern.

Families can then be divided into Genera (singular, Genus) and the Genera, finally into Species.

For our purposes we have defined a species as those plants that can and do interbreed to produce fertile offspring. We have ignored hybrids, sub-species and varieties.

Whenever we have used the term Family as outlined above, we have written it with a capital F. When we have used the term in a more colloquial way, then it is written 'family'.

Again, we must not forget that this is a man-made system imposed on nature.

Textbooks arrange the Families in an order based on their likely position in an evolutionary tree. The authors of the *Atlas* followed this sequence and we also have decided to follow it. Alphabetical sequence appears straightforward but this can put plants with very similar features well apart depending on names that humans have given them.

We have tried to restrict the use of 'botanical' terminology to an absolute minimum. Where it has been especially difficult to avoid its use, we hope that the photographs at the end of this section and in the main body of the book will go a long way to explaining it.

Since the users of this book will, we hope, range from absolute beginners to those with a sound knowledge, we hope that the latter group will not feel that they are being patronised by our explaining in the simplest terms.

In the circumstances, and with relatively few terms, we feel that it is easier to explain them under such headings as 'Flower Parts' rather than in the conventional alphabetical order.

Parts of a Plant
The Flower

Petals In many cases the petals are the 'shop window adverts' of the plant, evolved to attract insects. They are brightly coloured and often shaped to attract specific pollinators. In other cases, petals are either small or non-existent. This is particularly the case with wind pollinated plants; petals would be 'in the way'. The ring of petals is sometimes called the corolla.

Sepals These usually form a protective cup outside the petals. In a few plants they are coloured and re-inforce the attractiveness of the petals. The ring of sepals is called the calyx.

Stamen This consists of the anther which holds the pollen and the filament which is the stalk that holds the anther. This is the male part of the flower.

Carpel This is made up of the stigma, a pad to collect and hold the pollen, a style or stalk to hold the stigma and the ovary. This contains the ovules. The ovules become the seeds and the ovary becomes the fruit. This is the female part of the flower.

Fruit This is the outer case of the seeds. It may be juicy e.g. a grape, dry e.g. a pod or little more than a group of hooks e.g. a burr. It develops from the ovary wall.

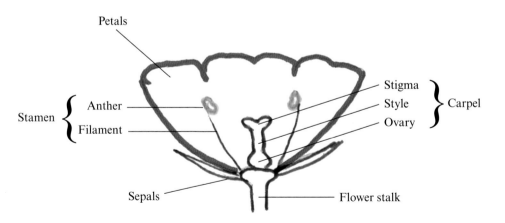

With many flowers, the various parts do not mature at the same time. Thus parts may seem to be missing or of a totally different size and shape. This is particularly the case with the carpels and the stamens. This 'staggering' of maturity reduces the likelihood of self-pollination.

Young flower.

Anthers ripe and bursting with pollen.

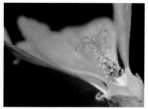

Stigma open to 'catch' pollen from another flower.

Other Parts of a Plant

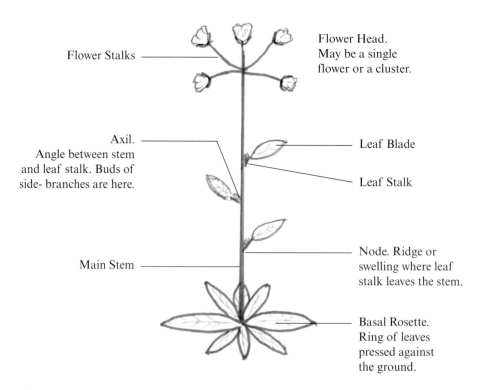

Flower Stalks

Flower Head.
May be a single
flower or a cluster.

Axil.
Angle between stem
and leaf stalk. Buds of
side- branches are here.

Leaf Blade

Leaf Stalk

Main Stem

Node. Ridge or
swelling where leaf
stalk leaves the stem.

Basal Rosette.
Ring of leaves
pressed against
the ground.

Parts of a Plant
Leaves

Node. This is the point at which the leaf stalk is attached to the stem.

Alternate is the term used when leaves come away from the stem on alternate sides i.e. one left and then one right and so on.

Opposite is the term used when leaves come away from the stem in opposite pairs.

The shapes of the leaves are best described by the illustrations.

Simple or entire

Toothed

Coarse toothed

Roundly lobed

Sharply lobed

Ivy-shaped

Heart-shaped

Palmate, like fingers from the palm

Pinnate

Finely divided

Whorled

Other terms

Stipules. Leaf-like structure usually growing out from the base of the leaf stalk.

Tendrils. Usually linked with the leaves. Long string-like growths which aid a plant to climb.

Umbel. This usually refers to the flower head and is when the head is made up of individual flowers held on stalks like the spokes of an umbrella.

Rhizome. A swollen stem which usually grows horizontally and either at ground level or just below the surface.

Bract. Sometimes called a 'dustbin' word. Any structure e.g. a scale which does not conventionally fit into a straightforward category is called a bract.

Size and Height

Photographs, particularly close-ups can give a misleading impression of the size of a plant. To help judge the size of a plant, a figure is quoted for the height. Unfortunately, when writing a precise figure, that too can be misleading. Some plants e.g. nettles all grow to about the same height but others such as dandelions have different growth forms. A dandelion growing amongst close cut grass will have a rosette of leaves which hug the ground and a flowering stem of 2 or 3 cms. The same plant growing amongst meadow grasses will have a tall rosette of leaves like a shuttlecock and a flowering stem of about 15 cms. Therefore, to write that the height varies from 2 to 15 cms is too vague to be helpful. The figure we have quoted for height is very much an average and it can be assumed that all the figures are prefixed with 'about'. The spread of plants, especially clump forming ones can be so varied that there seems little point in noting it.

In ordinary usage, the word tree is used to describe a plant which is tall (20 metres +) and with a distinct trunk. The words shrub or bush are used to describe something smaller (up to about 7 metres) and with a number of branches emerging from near to the ground. In reality, plants do not conform to this neat division and we all accept this when one person talks about a Holly bush another refers to a Holly tree.

In a handful of plants, where two species are closely related and are very similar in appearance, we have omitted photographs of one of the species and described, in the text, the way in which they can be differentiated.

THE BAY FAMILY   LAURACEAE

There is only one member of this Family recorded in the *Atlas*.

Bay   Laurus nobilis (AP 12)

Evergreen shrub with strong distinctive smell. Flowers creamy white, about 1 cm across.
Leaves oval, glossy-green with wrinkled edge. Fruit (on female tree) a dark purple berry.
Height - 10 metres

THE WATER-LILY FAMILY   NYMPHAEACEAE

Aquatic plants with at least some large floating leaves. Flowers cup shaped.

White Water-lily   Nymphaea alba (AP 12)

Large white flowers
(20 cms across)
Large floating leaves
Height - grows on the water surface

Yellow Water-lily   Nuphar lutea (AP 12)

Small (7 cms) yellow flowers.   Distinctive shaped pod.
Has both submerged and floating leaves. *Height - grows on the water surface.*

N.B. Fringed Water-lily also has yellow flowers but the petals are fringed and have
a triangular darker yellow centre. It is not classed as a member of the Water-lily family
(See P221)

THE HORNWORT FAMILY   CERATOPHYLLACEAE

Submerged aquatics with whorls of finely divided leaves.
Flowers solitary and minute.

Rigid Hornwort
Ceratophyllum demersum (AP 12)

Terminal leaves form a bushy head.
Leaves fork once (or rarely twice).
The stem is very brittle.
Length - 1.5 metres

Soft Hornwort
Ceratophyllum submersum   (AP 13)

Leaves fork three to four times.
Leaves and stem are soft.
Length - 1 metre.

THE BUTTERCUP FAMILY   RANUNCULACEAE

Many members of this Family have petals which form the "traditional" cup. Also, many members have yellow petals. However, other members of this family have petals which form a complicated pattern and they may not be yellow.

What they do have in common is a flower with many stamens and numerous seed pods all with the same basic pattern. Most have 4 to 6 petals and few in the Family exceed 1 metre in height.

The Family can be divided into two sections;

1) Those that have the traditional flower. There are 13 species in this group.
2) Those species that have the stamens and seed pods of the Family but do not have the yellow cups. The Crowfoot group have cup-shaped petals but they are white. Others in this section include Hellebores, Anemones, Clematis, Meadow-rues, Love-in-a-mist, Columbine, Monkshood, Wolfbane, Larkspur and Mousetail.

Columbine flower   Columbine seed pod   Clematis flower   Clematis seed pod

Those with yellow cups

The first four traditional buttercup types are the common ones and most likely to be found.

Lesser Celandine   **Ranunculus ficaria (AP 17)**

Has 8/10 petals which turn white as they age. Leaves are heart shaped and often mottled. Flowers in very early spring. They are not closely related to Greater Celandine. *Height - 10 cms*

Creeping Buttercup   **Ranunculus repens (AP 15)**

Spreads by runners and forms a mat. Leaves divided into three lobes, often with pale markings on the lobes. Stems are furrowed and hairy. *Height - 20 cms*

Bulbous Buttercup   **Ranunculus bulbosus (AP 15)**

Sepals are sharply turned back along the stem. The leaves are divided into three lobes and the terminal lobe has its own distinct 'stem' Stems are furrowed and hairy and swollen at the base. The Hairy, Small-flowered and Celery-leaved species also have turned back sepals but are distinguished as their names suggest. *Height - 50 cms*

THE BUTTERCUP FAMILY Cont'd

Meadow or Field Buttercup   <u>Ranunculus acris</u> (AP 15)

Leaf often divided into
five branched segments.

Tall, up to 80 cms.   *Height - 80 cms*   Stem not furrowed,
hairy.

'Buttercup' type flowers which are either rare or limited
to less common habitats, (see *Atlas*)

Hairy Buttercup   <u>Ranunculus sardous</u> (AP 16)

Very like Bulbous Buttercup but markedly more hairy.
Has turned back sepals.

Flowers pale yellow. More
noticeable when seen in a mass.
The upper leaves have long,
narrow leaflets.

Height - 30 cms

Goldilocks Buttercup   <u>Ranunculus auricomus</u> (AP 16)

Irregular petal numbers, they vary from 3 - 6. Leaf divided into five long, thin leaflets;
basal leaves broader. *Height - 30 cms*

THE BUTTERCUP FAMILY Cont'd

Corn Buttercup   Ranunculus arvensis (AP 16)

Spiny fruits. Small flowers about 1 cm across). Smooth stem.
Height 40 cms

Small-flowered Buttercup   Ranunculus parviflorus (AP 16)

Flowers very small (5 mm across)
Flowers pale with yellow sepals that appear
to project beyond the petals.
Leaves with 3 toothed-lobes.
This plant seems to have become scarcer
in the last few years.
Height 25cms

Celery-leaved Buttercup   Ranunculus sceleratus (AP 16)

 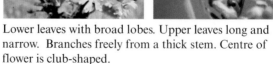 

Grows in fresh water
on muddy banks.
Height - 60 cms

Lower leaves with broad lobes. Upper leaves long and
narrow. Branches freely from a thick stem. Centre of
flower is club-shaped.

16

THE BUTTERCUP FAMILY Cont'd

Lesser Spearwort

Grows in wet acidic soil. Flowers about 10mms across. The petals are spaced from each other.
Height 25 cms

Ranunculus flammula (AP 17)

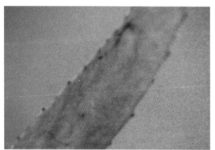

Leaves 60mms long and spear shaped. Lower leaves often have small teeth.

Seed pods without hooks.

Greater Spearwort

Leaves up to 20cms in length.
Height - 100cms

Ranunculus lingua (AP 16)

Flowers about 30mms across petals overlap. Grows near water.

Seed pods have small hooks.

THE BUTTERCUP FAMILY Cont'd

Marsh-marigold   (King-cups)

This looks like a typical buttercup but the 'petals' are really sepals. This is most noticeable in the opening buds.

Seed pod is star-like.

Caltha palustris (AP 13)

Leaves are kidney shaped and finely toothed near the leaf stalk.

Sepals turn white as they age.

Winter Aconite

Usually has 6 petals. Flowers very early in the year.
Height - 15cms

Eranthis hyemalis (AP 14)

Has distinctive frill of green leaves and palmate lower ones.

THE BUTTERCUP FAMILY Cont'd

Flowers that are not typical 'buttercup' for either shape or colour.

Water Crowfoots   **(AP 17 & 18)**

These have the typical cup shape but the petals are white, sometimes with small yellow markings. Because they grow in water, or on mud, they are often difficult to approach closely. We have, therefore, followed the system of dividing them into only three groups.
1) Those with all the leaves floating on the water surface.
2) Those with some floating and some submerged leaves.
3) Those with only submerged leaves.

Group 1

All the leaves are floating on the water/mud surface.

The individual species are:- Ivy-leaved crowfoot;   Ranunculus hederaceus
                                 Round-leaved crowfoot;   Ranunculus omiophyllus

Group 2

The members of this group have both floating and submerged leaves. The floating leaves of the common one are rounded and toothed whilst the floating leaves of the other two species are almost trefoil.

The underwater leaves are thread-like.

The individual species are:- Common Water-crowfoot;   Ranunculus aquatilis
                                   Pond Water-crowfoot;   Ranunculus peltatus
                                   Brackish Water-crowfoot;   Ranunculus baudotii

THE BUTTERCUP FAMILY Cont'd

<u>Group 3</u>

In this group, the plants have only submerged leaves. In fast flowing streams, the thread-like leaves are "combed" by the water current.

The individual species are:- Fan-leaved Water-crowfoot; Ranunculus circinatus
                  Thread-leaved Water-crowfoot; Ranunculus trichophyllus
                  Stream Water-crowfoot; Ranunculus penicillatus

Should the reader wish to determine exactly which species is present we suggest referring to either. *Wild Flowers* by Fitter, Fitter and Blamey or *New Flora of the British Isles* by Stace.

Hellebores   Land plants with green/purple/white flowers.

<u>Green Hellebore</u>   **<u>Helleborus viridis (AP 13)</u>**

Flowers are open green cups with five fleshy green petals. Leaves toothed and palmate. Flowering stems unbranched and emerge from base of the plant. *Height 50 cms*

<u>Stinking Hellebore</u>   **<u>Helleborus foetidus (AP 13)</u>**

Flowers form barely opened cups. Petals are greenish-yellow edged with purple. Leaves palmate with narrow toothed leaflets. *Height 1 metre*

THE BUTTERCUP FAMILY Cont'd

Lenten-rose

Helleborus orientalis (AP 14)

Flowers with five petals in an open cup about 5 cms across. Petals usually off-white with purple markings.

Leaves palmate with 3 to 7 finely toothed leaflets.
Height 30 cms

Anemones   Flat rather than cup-shaped flowers.

Japanese Anemone

Anemone x hybrida (AP 15)

The only tall (1 metre plus) member of this group

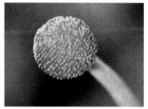

Has five pink or white large petals; petals have a notch on the top edge. After petal fall, the head looks like a pin-cushion. Leaves are lobed.
Height 1.5+ metres

Wood Anemone

Anemone nemorosa (AP 15)

Flower with six narrowish white petals. Leaves much divided. Flowers solitary, one on each stem. Flowers in early Spring.
Height 15 cms

THE BUTTERCUP FAMILY Cont'd

Yellow Anemone
Anemone ranunculoides (AP 15)

Flowers similar to Wood Anemone but yellow and slightly smaller. Typically five petals rather than six. *Height - 15 cms*

Blue Anemone
Anemone apennina (AP 15)

This should not be confused with blue Anemone blanda - often grown in gardens.

Flowers usually blue, but can be pink or white. Petals numerous. *Height - 10 cms*

Petals downy on the underside. (A. blanda is not downy).

Clematis Group

Woody perennial climbers.

Traveller's-joy / Old-man's-beard
Clematis vitalba   (AP 15)

A woody climber with trusses of creamy white flowers. Flowers with four "petals" about 12mm across.

Seed heads have white/grey feathery plumes.

Height 5+ metres

Leaves in pairs and the leaf stalk twists around suitable support.

THE BUTTERCUP FAMILY Cont'd

Himalayan Clematis

Flowers with four white or pink petals.
Flowers about 3 cms across.
Height - 5+ metres

Purple Clematis

Flowers purple. *Height - 4+ metres*

Clematis montana (AP 15)

Leaf divided into three leaflets.
It is the leaf stalk which twists around
the support.

Clematis viticella (AP 15)

Seed head without feathery plumes.

The remainder of the Buttercup family are very unlike the common Buttercup. However, they are each very distinctive in their own way and need only a brief written description to supplement the photographs.

Common Meadow-rue

Small creamy-white flowers in dense
clusters. Petals are small and white; the
creamy colour comes from the stamens.
Height - 80cms

Thalictrum flavum (AP 19)

Leaves with toothed leaflets. At a
distance, Meadow-rue is not unlike
Meadowsweet, the leaves however are
very different. See page 140.

THE BUTTERCUP FAMILY Cont'd

Lesser Meadow-rue   Thalictrum minus (AP 19)

Stems thin and 'twiggy'.
Very small flowers in open
clusters.
Height - 60 cms

Leaves very branched,
leaflets slightly toothed.

Love-in-a-mist   Nigella damascena (AP 14)

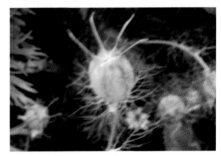

Flowers usually pale blue, but white and,
very rarely, pink forms occur. Fine outgrowths (bracts) below the flower give it
the 'mist'.

Bladder-like seed pod.
Height - 40 cms

Columbine   Aquilegia vulgaris (AP 18)

Flowers are in clusters, each flower made up of five
petals gathered to form a tube and a spur. Usually
purple/blue but pink forms do occur.
Height - 60 cms

Seed pods typical of the
Family.

THE BUTTERCUP FAMILY Cont'd

Monk's-hood

Aconitum napellus (AP 14)

Deep purple
flowers, each with
distinctive hood.
Leaves divided;
stems slightly
downy.
Height - 1 metre

Larkspur

Consolida ajacis   (AP 15)

Five petalled
blue flowers with
distinct spur at
the back.
Leaves very
divided.
Height - 50 cms

Mousetail

Myosurus minimus (AP 18)

Flowers with very
small green/yellow
petals, are carried
on a slender spike.
Height - 10 cms

THE BARBERRY FAMILY   BERBERIDACEAE

Apart from the Barrenwort, this family is made up of shrubs with trusses of yellow flowers. They are spiky with the spines either on the leaves (Oregon Grape) or on the stems, or both.

Barren-wort or Bishop's-hat   Epimedium alpinum (AP 19)

Low growing mat forming perennial. Flowers have four yellow/red petals and four sepals. Leaves are heart shaped and usually marbled or with coloured veins.
Height - 15 cms

Oregon-grape   Mahonia aquifolium (AP 20)

Leaves made up of 5 or 6 pairs of spiny edged leaflets. Leaves often show 'Autumn colours' early in the year. Leaves grow close together at the top of the stem giving a 'rosette' appearance; the flower spike comes from the centre of this rosette.

Fruits blue/purple and grape-like.   *Height -3 metres*

THE BARBERRY FAMILY Cont'd

The flowers of the Barberry plants (see pages 27 and 28) are all very similar.
The leaves, spines and fruits are all significant in identifying the species.

Hedge Barberry

Young stems droop
downwards.
Height - 3 metres

Berberis x stenophylla (AP 20)

Leaves narrow and about 15 mms long with silky down
on the underside. Has three short spines with the largest
in the centre.

Darwin's Barberry

Berberis darwinii (AP 20)

Flowers are deep rich
yellow/orange.

Leaves are small
and holly-like.

Short stem spines are in
groups of five.

Fruits are blue/purple.

Height - 2 metres

Barberry

Flowers in short clusters.

Height - 3 metres

Berberis vulgaris (AP 19)

Fruit is oval-shaped and red.

Long spines in threes
and leaves spoon shaped.

THE BARBERRY FAMILY Cont'd

Chinese Barberry   Berberis julianae (AP 20)

Leaves leathery, shiny and oval with about eight or more spines on each side; leaves about 10 cms long. Has three long stem spines. Fruits oval, turning black when ripe.
Height - 2 metres

Gagnepain's Barberry   Berberis gagnepainii (AP 19)

Leaves are thin, oval with spiny edges, and up to 10 cms long. Three long stem spines. Fruit oval. Red at first, then turning purple/black.
Height - 2 metres

Mrs Wilson's Barberry   Berberis wilsoniae (AP 19)

Leaves about 2cms long, oval and broadest to the tip. Leaves about 2cms long. Long spines in threes. Fruit is green ripening to pink.
Height - 3 metres

THE BARBERRY FAMILY Cont'd

Great Barberry   Berberis glaucocarpa (AP 19)

This is only recorded as an introduced species and occurs chiefly around Porlock.
The leaves are broadish and toothed and the flowers are pale yellow.
Height 3 metres

THE POPPY FAMILY   PAPAVERACEAE

Typically, the members of this family have four papery petals.
The best known examples are red but some species show a range of colours.
Outside the petals they have two sepals but these rarely persist.
Most of them have a single flower at the end of an un-branched stem.
When damaged they secrete a white or yellow juice.
The seed pods also have features which help in identification.

Large (tall) plants

Oriental Poppy   Papaver orientale (AP 20)

A tall plant with very large flowers (10 cms across) Petals usually red with dark centre. Leaves roughly hairy almost pinnate, and toothed.
Height - 1.5metres

THE POPPY FAMILY Cont'd

Opium Poppy   Papaver somniferum (AP 21)

Another large poppy with flowers up to 10 cms across. Petals usually lilac/purple but variants do exist. Leaves fleshy. The seed pods function like pepper pots.

Height - 1.5 metres

Red flowered Poppies

The following poppies are red flowered and, in general, resemble the traditional poppy. The presence, or absence, of a dark spot at the base of the petals is an unreliable guide to identification. The shape of the seed pod is often a more useful guide.

Common Poppy   Papaver rhoeas (AP 21)

Petals usually have a dark centre. Seed pod is smooth, oval/round with a flat top. Stem is bristly. *Height - 60 cms*

Long-headed Poppy   Papaver dubium (AP 21)

Petals usually without dark centre, flower about 4 - 5cms across.
Height - 50 cms

Seed pod long, slender and rigid on a long stem.

THE POPPY FAMILY Cont'd

Rough Poppy

Papaver hybridum (AP 21)

A simple red flower, rough leaves but a distinctive seed pod. *Height - 40 cms*

Poppies with yellow/orange petals

Atlas Poppy

Papaver atlanticum (AP 20)

Has four orange petals which form an open cross. Leaves are lobed. The dead Carpel remains like a beak at the top of the seed pod. *Height - 60 cms*

Welsh Poppy

Meconopsis cambrica (AP 21)

Leaf much divided, sometimes pinnate.

Petals are pale yellow and overlap each other. *Height - 60 cms*

The seed head is a narrow oval shape.

THE POPPY FAMILY Cont'd

Californian Poppy

Petals usually orange but can range from pale yellow to red. Seed head long and thin.

Eschscholzia californica (AP 22)

Leaves much divided into narrow leaflets.
Height 30 cms

Yellow Horned - poppy

Leaves silvery grey. Sprawling growth on shingle.

Glaucium flavum (AP 22)

Very long, narrow curved seed pod.
Height 50 cms

Yellow-juiced Poppy

Flowers are smaller (about 3-4 cms) than those of the Yellow Horned-poppy but it has the same very long slender seed pods.

Papaver dubium (a sub species) (AP 21)

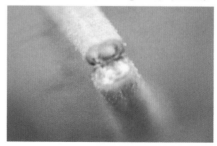

Stem gives off a yellow juice if damaged.
Height 40 cms

THE POPPY FAMILY Cont'd

Greater Celandine   Chelidonium majus (AP 22)

Petals form a yellow cross. Stem is branched and leaves are shaped like oak-leaves.
Sepals have long hairs. Seed pod is beaded.
Height 60 cms

THE FUMITORY FAMILY   FUMARIACEAE

The flowers of this family are
tube-shaped with two lips at the front
and a spur at the back.
The leaves are usually much divided.
The family can be divided into two
groups - those with non-purple flowers
and those whose flowers are
predominantly purple/pink.

Non-purple species

Yellow Corydalis   Pseudofumaria lutea (AP 23)

Flowers bright yellow.
Flowers in loose clusters of about eight at
the top of the stem.
Leaves divided and delicate looking.
Height - 40 cms

Pale Corydalis   Pseudofumaria alba   (AP 23)

Very like Yellow Corydalis
but has creamy-white
flowers with yellow/green
tips to the lips.
Flower stalk slightly winged.
Height -30 cms

THE FUMITORY FAMILY Cont'd

Climbing Corydalis   Ceratocapnos claviculata   (AP 23)

Flowers pale yellow in small clusters. Scrambling growth habit to about one metre. Leaves end in a tendril.
Height - 1 metre

Fern-leaved Corydalis   Corydalis cheilanthifolia   (AP 22)

Leaves much divided, fern-like. Flowers yellow in a longish spike. Flowers curved, banana-shaped.
Height - 15 cms

White Ramping-fumitory   Fumaria capreolata   (AP 23)

Flowers creamy-white tipped with purple. Has a greenish ridge running on the top of the flower. Sepals toothed. Scrambling growth habit.
Height - climbing to 1 metre

Pink - Purple members of the family

The details of the flowers are best shown by the photographs.

Bleeding-heart   Dicentra formosa   (AP 22)

Distinctive shape of the flowers separate it from the rest of the Family. Heart-shaped flowers hanging in a row from an arching stem. Flowers in shades of white and pink. Flower stem is leafless.
Height - 50 cms

THE FUMITORY FAMILY Cont'd

Common Ramping-fumitory   Fumaria muralis   (AP 23)

The mature flower spike is about the same length as the rest of the flower stalk.
Sepals are toothed near the base. The flower tube is pinkish-white with a purplish
blotch at the tip. Seed case is smooth.
Height 40 cms

Tall Ramping-fumitory   Fumaria bastardii   (AP 23)

Very similar to Common Ramping Fumitory. It is distinguished by the fact that the
floral part of the spike is longer than the rest of the stalk. The sepals are toothed
along all the edge.

Common Fumitory   Fumaria officinalis   (AP 24)

Leaves are silvery/grey.
(another name for the plant
is Smoke-bush).
Height - 40 cms

The flowering spike is
longer than the stalk.

Flowers 6 - 7 mm long and
the upperlip is dark purple.

THE FUMITORY FAMILY Cont'd

Bird-in-a-bush

Low growing with fleshy leaves.
Height - 15 cms

Corydalis solida   (AP 22)

Flower spur is down-turned in early
growth but straightens as it matures.

Leaf stalks have
scale at the base.

LONDON PLANE FAMILY   PLATANACEAE

Despite its common name, the London Plane is not a member of the true Plane family;
it is the only local member of this family.

London Plane   Platanus x hispanica   (AP 24)

Bark peels very frequently.   Leaves are sharply lobed.

The outer seed case is a
hanging spiky globe.

Height 30 metres

THE ELM FAMILY   ULMACEAE

The leaves of this family all appear 'lop-sided'

English Elm   ## Ulmus procera   (AP 25)

Rows of stately Elms, which were common throughout the country were affected in the late 1960s by Dutch Elm disease. Some root stocks remained alive and put up suckers.

Typically these suckers grows to between 5 and 7 metres and then they too become affected and die back. Leaves up to 10 cms and the surface feels rough. Twigs often have a corky bark. Now rare as a mature tree. The seed case is oval and with the seed near one edge. *Height - 30 metres*

Wych Elm   ## Ulmus glabra   (AP 24)

Height - 40 metres   Has the largest leaves, up   Seed case is round with the
                          to 15 cms, with rough upper   seed in the centre.
                          surface. Leaf stalk is very
                          short.

THE HEMP FAMILY   CANNABACEAE

The members of this family have inconspicuous green/yellow flowers.
The male and female flowers are on separate plants. Leaves palmately lobed.

Hemp

Leaves divided into long, narrow,
spray-like leaflets.
Height - 2 metres

Cannabis sativa (AP 25)

Flower head made up of a cluster of
pale green flowers held in the angle of
the stem and the leaf stalk. It is illegal
to propagate this plant.

Hop

Rambling climber, typically in hedgerows.

Leaf with 3 - 5 leaflets.
Height - 10 metres

Humulus lupulus (AP 25)

Small flowers in a drooping truss.

Cluster of drying heads.

THE FIG FAMILY   MORACEAE

Trees or shrubs producing edible fruit. Although it is a member of this Family, the *Atlas* does not recognise any Mulberry tree as "wild".

Fig   Ficus carica (AP 25)

Palmate leaf of classical shape. Edible somewhat pear-shaped fruit.
Height - 10 metres. Near walls

THE NETTLE FAMILY   URTICACEAE

Mind-your-own-business   Soleirolia soleirolii (AP 26)

Usually grows as a ground-hugging low (2 cms) mat on damp ground near walls. Leaves alternate, small and oval/round. Flowers very small, pink. *Height - 2 cms*

Pellitory-of-the-wall   Parietaria judaica (AP 26)

Almost always on walls. Leaves alternate. Flowers very small, ripening to reddish fruits.
Height - spreads along a wall (20 cms) in a low mat (5 cms) pressed against the wall.

THE NETTLE FAMILY Cont'd….

Common Nettle   Urtica dioica (AP 25)

The well known stinging nettle.
Flowers in loose trusses.
Leaves opposite, coarsely toothed
and stinging.
Prefers moist rich shady soil.
Height 1.5 metres

Small Nettle   Urtica urens (AP 25)

A shorter (50 cms) nettle.
Leaves opposite, and a brighter green.
Garden weed.
Height 50 cms

THE WALNUT TREE FAMILY   JUGLANDACEAE

There is only one member of this Family present as a Wild tree.

Walnut Tree   Juglans regia (AP 26)

Pinnate leaf divided into 7 leaflets. The leaves are pointed
at the tip but not toothed. The flowers (catkins) open at
the same time as the leaves open. The nut (shell and
kernel) are enclosed in a slightly fleshy outer case.
Height - 30 metres

THE MYRTLE FAMILY

MYRICACEAE

Bog-myrtle

Myrica gale (AP 26)

Shrub whose leaves give off distinctive scent. Plants are single sexed. Flowers are orange-brown catkins which emerge before the leaves open. Leaves oval, about 4 cms long.
Height - 2 metres

THE BEECH FAMILY

FAGACEAE

Includes -
Beech
Southern Beech (Nothofagus)
Sweet Chestnut
Oaks

Trees with shiny green leaves born alternately along the twig.

Beech

Fagus sylvatica (AP 26)

In Winter, the trunks are a smooth elephant-grey. The leaves which are lopsided at the base, form a dense mosaic. The young buds are cigar shaped. The fruit (nuts) are three sided and carried in a four sided spiky case.
Height - 30 metres

Nothofagus group

These are deciduous trees from the Southern Hemisphere which look something like the European Beech. The leaves are alternate and the fruits are like small Beech nuts.

THE BEECH FAMILY Cont'd

Sweet Chestnut   Castanea sativa (AP 27)

Trunk has spiral ridges.
The flowers are clustered and look like a yellow shuttle-cock. The leaves are toothed and grow close together and appear almost palmate. The edible fruit (chestnuts) are formed in a case covered with hair like bristles.
Height - 30 metres

Oak Trees

The male and female flowers are separate but born on the same tree. The male flowers are catkins producing pollen and the female produces the acorns. The acorns, their cups and the leaves are a better guide to identification than are the flowers.

Evergreen (Holm or Holly) Oak   Quercus ilex (AP 27)

The bark is very dark and cracks into small squares. Upper surface of the leaves is dark and glossy. The tree is evergreen.
Height - 30 metres

Acorns are well enclosed in the cups. The outer skin of the cup looks as if it was "engine turned".

Lucombe Oak   Quercus xpseudosuber (AP 27)

A semi evergreen tree - old leaves fall off after new growth has started. Older leaves have a brown edge. Bark is corky. The Acorn cups have finger-like outgrowths.
Height - 30 metres

THE BEECH FAMILY Cont'd

Red Oak   Quercus rubra (AP 28)

A deciduous tree.
The leaves have sharp pointed lobes.
Height - 25 metres

After first year, acorns look like
doughnuts; they fill out in the 2nd year.

Turkey Oak   Quercus cerris (AP 27)

Deciduous. Leaves small about 7 cms long.
Lobes pronounced and almost pointed.
Height - 40 metres

The acorns are slender, almost pointed
and with a noticeable tip. The acorn cup
has fringe like outgrowth.

Pedunculate Oak   Quercus robur (AP 28)

Deciduous; the typical
'English' oak. Branches
usually curved or bent.
Height - 30 metres

Leaves on very short stalks.

Rounded acorns on
long stalks.

43

THE BEECH FAMILY Cont'd

Sessile Oak   Quercus petraea   (AP 27)

Deciduous; often forms 'scrub' oak.
Leaves on a short, but noticeable, stalk.
Height - 30 metres

Acorns without stalks. The acorns are
oval and the cups are scaly.

Cork Oak   Quercus suber   (AP 28)

Evergreen. Only one specimen recorded in the *Atlas*. Very thick corky bark. Leaves short,
6 cms long, slightly toothed; tend to curl back on themselves. Acorn cups quite thick.
Height - 20 metres

THE BIRCH FAMILY   BETULAEAE

The Family includes:-   Birch, Alder, Hornbeam, Hazel

Birch Trees

Trees with a light foliage and bark which becomes white/silver with age. Separate male and
female flowers are born on the same tree. The male flowers are in the form of catkins.

Silver Birch   Betula pendula   (AP 28)

  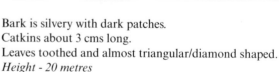

Bark is silvery with dark patches.
Catkins about 3 cms long.
Leaves toothed and almost triangular/diamond shaped.
Height - 20 metres

THE BIRCH FAMILY Cont'd

Downy Birch   Betula pubescens   (AP 28)

Bark pale grey with dark   Young twigs are downy.   Long catkins, opening early
patches. Usually grows in   Leaves toothed and rounded   in the year.
wet/damp conditions.   at the base.   *Height - 20 metres*

Alder

Trees, usually growing near water. The fruits are cone-like.

Alder   Alnus glutinosa   (AP 28)

Leaves have seven pairs of veins and are   Fruit is an egg shaped 'cone' about
notched at the tip. Male catkins are long   2 cms long.
- about 10 cms.   *Height - 20 metres*

Grey Alder   Alnus incana   (AP 29)

Leaf is slightly lobed, toothed and   Long male catkins - about 10 cms. Fruit
pointed at the tip; the leaf of the   are 'cones' about 1 cms long.
Common Alder ends in a small groove.   *Height - 20 metres*
Leaves have up to twelve pairs of downy
veins on the underside.

THE BIRCH FAMILY Cont'd

Hornbeam   Carpinus betulus   (AP 29)

Flower in the form
of a catkin.
Height - 20 metres

Leaves oval and toothed with 9 -12 pairs of parallel veins.
The pods are pale green with a "Chinese pagoda"
appearance.

Hazel   Corylus avellana   (AP 29)

Leaves round with small teeth
and pointed tips. Often coppiced
to form multiple trunks.

Long male catkins,
6-8 cms.

Fruit is hazel nut.
Height - 5 metres

THE POKEWEED FAMILY   PHYTOLACCACEAE

The only local member of this family is a rare herbaceous perennial, best described by
the photographs.

Indian Pokeweed   Phytolacca acinosa   (AP 29)

Leaves long (30 cms) and oval,
coming to a point at the tip.

Flower pink. Branching stem.
Height - 2 metres

THE GOOSEFOOT FAMILY   CHENOPODIACEAE

Leaves usually alternate. Flowers small and greenish, usually in a cluster along the flower spike. Petals and sepals (if present) usually in one combined whorl.

The family includes the following members -
Saltwort, Glasswort, Sea-blite, Sea Beet, Orache and Goosefoot.

Prickly Saltwort   Salsola kali (AP 33)

Prickly
coastal plant.
Leaves fleshy and
tipped with a spine.
Sprawling
growth habit.
Height - 50 cms

Glassworts or Marsh Samphire

Succulent, edible plants which grow on salt marshes.

Because they grow on slippy estuarine clay/mud it is often impractical to get close to them. As a group they can be identified quite easily, but to separate out the species involves close inspection. Features such as colour, degree of branching etc help in identification but to be certain one needs to make a close inspection of the flower. They flower towards the end of summer and the flowers are very small; a hand lens is needed to see them in detail.

For these reasons, we have treated this group under their general name.

As a rough guide to the individual species, two of which are very rare, we add the table below.

Common Glasswort	-	Bright green	-	Joints not swollen or waisted.
Purple Glasswort	-	Turquoise red/purple	-	Much branched
One flowered Glasswort (very rare)	-	Turns red/purple	-	Joints slightly swollen. Small side branches.
Long-spiked Glasswort (very rare)	-	Turns brown	-	Joints not waisted.

Common Glasswort

Erect, bright green
branches.
Joints not swollen
or waisted.
Three small flowers
across the stem,
the central one
being the largest.
Height - 40 cms

Salicornia europaea   (AP 33)

Annual Sea-blite (Sea-blight)

Suaeda maritima   (AP 33)

Annual with reddish stem. Leaves grey/green and cylindrical. Flowers insignificant.
Turns purple/red. Occurs in salt marshes.
Height - 30 cms

Sea Beet

Beta vulgaris   (AP 32)

Coarse, spreading perennial. Flowers on long spikes. Grows on coastal mud sites. Lower
leaves almost triangular, upper leaves more grass like. Leaves darkish green and shiny.
Height - 75 cms

THE GOOSEFOOT FAMILY Cont'd...

Oraches

Separate male and female flowers on the same plant. Have scale-like bracts at the base of the flower spikes. Leaves vary in shape; the higher up the stem, the simpler the shape.

Sea Purslane

A shrub. Leaves mealy and oval.
Height - 1 metre

Atriplex portulacoides (AP 32)

Prominent yellow stamens give flower distinctive appearance.

Grass-leaved Orache

Leaves grass-like, sometimes slightly toothed. Side veins faint. Bracts, at the base of the flowers, without stalks.
Height - 80 cms

Atriplex littoralis (AP 32)

Frosted Orache

Generally low growing. Leaves silvery and with rounded lobes.

Atriplex laciniata (AP 32)

Upper leaves less lobed.
Height - 30 cms

THE GOOSEFOOT FAMILY Cont'd...

Garden Orache   Atriplex hortensis   (AP 31)

This rare casual has red stems and leaves.
Height - 2 metres

Leaves are rounded triangles.

Bracts are rounded/oval.

Spear-leaved Orache   Atriplex prostrata   (AP 31)

Leaves variable: commonly triangular with three lobes, the bottom two pointing out at right angles or even downwards. Occasionally leaves are triangular with a wavy edge. Stems sometimes reddish.
Height - 1 metre

Babington's Orache   Atriplex glabriuscula   (AP 31)

Similar to Spear-leaved but more mealy. Prostrate growth habit. Leaves are toothed and diamond shaped. *Height - 1 metre*

THE GOOSEFOOT FAMILY Cont'd...

Common Orache

Atriplex patula (AP 32)

Very variable.
Leaves with three
lobes; the two
lateral ones
pointing forwards.
Leaf gradually
broadens out from
leaf stalk.
Height - 1 metre

Goosefoot group

The members of this group have tiny, petal-less flowers. The flowers are in spikes. Male and female flowers are on the same flower head. Identification is easier if the leaf shape is examined; but leaf shape does vary! Fat-hen is a common and widespread Goosefoot. Probably it is easier to work along the following sequence and eliminate as appropriate.

Fat-hen

Chenopodium album (AP 31)

Lower leaves oval and
toothed; middle and upper
leaves three lobed to spear
shaped.

Flower
heads
whitish.
Stem
goes
purple
with age.

Height - 1 metre

Good-king-henry

Chenopodium bonus-henricus (AP 30)

The only perennial in the group.
Flower spikes with a few or no
leaves between the flowers.
Leaves triangular with small
pointed lobes.
Height - 50 cms

51

THE GOOSEFOOT FAMILY Cont'd...

Many-seeded Goosefoot

Flowers in leafy spikes.
Height - 1 metre

Chenopodium polyspermum (AP 30)

Leaves oval and without side lobes.

Red Goosefoot

Leaves sharply toothed.
Leaves and flowers reddish as they ripen.
Flowers in compact spikes.
Height - 80 cms

Chenopodium rubrum (AP 30)

Fig-leaved Goosefoot

Chenopodium ficifolium (AP 30)

Similar to Fat Hen but leaves lobed rather
than toothed. Does not go reddish-purple
as it matures.
Height - 80 cms

THE PIGWEED FAMILY   AMARANTHACEAE

A Family with small insignificant flowers but they are arranged in large numbers in tassels which makes them quite showy. The lower leaves have leaf stalks, the upper leaves do not.

Love-lies-bleeding   **Amaranthus caudatus   (AP 33)**

Flowers in long drooping tassels, usually red or yellow. *Height - 40 cms*

Common Amaranth   **Amaranthus retroflexus   (AP 33)**

Tassels of green flowers held upright. Shiny, bristly bracts (scales) amongst the tassels. *Height - 80 cms*

THE PURSLANE FAMILY   PORTULACACEAE

Despite their name, Sea, Iceland, Hampshire and Water Purslane do not belong to this Family. Flowers only have two sepals (opposite to each other).

Springbeauty   **Claytonia perfoliata   (AP 34)**

The upper leaves are fused in pairs so that the stem appears to emerge from the middle of the leaves. Once above the leaves, the stem branches several times. Flower has four or five small white petals. *Height - 25 cms*

Pink Purslane

Claytonia sibirica   (AP 34)

Five notched petals. Flower stalks rise from pair of unfused leaves.
Leaves round with a small pointed tip. *Height - 30 cms*

Blinks

Montia fontana   (AP 34)

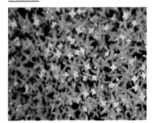

Flowers white and very small.
Flower stalks rise from pair of
unfused leaves. Leaves round with
a small pointed tip.
*Height - 20 cms, but can form
low mat.*

THE PINK FAMILY

CARYOPHYLLACEAE

The members have narrowish leaves in pairs. The stem is swollen at the leaf joints. The
leaves do not have leaf stalks and they are un-toothed. Petals in groups of five or multi-
ples of five. This Family can be divided into two groups:-

Group 1

The members of this group have largish (1 cm or more) flowers and most of them are
pink. The sepals of most are fused to form a tube. In some species, this tube, when
mature, swells to form a bladder. Members of this group include Pinks, Campions,
Ragged Robin, Corncockle.

Ragged Robin

Lychnis flos-cuculi   (AP 40)

Five deeply divided
deep pink petals,
(hence 'ragged').
Flowers about 4
cms across. Leaves
very narrow, mostly
at the base of the
reddish stems.
Height - 60 cms

THE PINK FAMILY Cont'd...

Corncockle

Agrostemma githago (AP 40)

Long straight stems. Seedling has opposite leaves giving 'cross' shape.
Five slightly notched deep pink petals. Flowers about 4 - 5 cms across.
Long thin sepals project between and beyond the petals. *Height - 1 metre*

Soapwort

Saponaria officinalis (AP 41)

Fleshy stem with narrow oval
pointed leaves. Flowers in a head.
Petals pale pink, or white
un-notched and 2 - 3 cms across.
Petal tube narrow. Double form
sometimes occurs.

Height - 50 cms

Rose Campion

Lychnis coronaria (AP 40)

Bright magenta flowers
with a whitish centre about
1.5 cms across. Leaves
woolly and grey.
Height - 50 cms

Red Campion

Silene dioica (AP 41)

Somewhat scrambling
growth. Bright pink
notched petals; flowers
about 2 cms across.
Leaves broadly oval tapering to a point at the tip.
Height - 1 metre

THE PINK FAMILY Cont'd...

White Campion   Silene latifolia   (AP 41)

Flowers white.
Height - 80 cms

Plant slightly less robust, and less sprawling than Red Campion.

Sepals form a brown veined slim bladder.

Bladder Campion   Silene vulgaris   (AP 40)

White deeply notched petals; flowers 2 cms across. Ring of sepals forms the swollen bladder. Leaves grey/green with fringe of fine hairs.
Height - 80 cms

Sea Campion   Silene uniflora   (AP 40)

Often forms a mat. Similar to Bladder Campion but leaves narrower and anthers darker. Bladder formed from the sepals is clearly veined and sometimes pink.
Height - 40 cms

Berry Catchfly   Cucubalus baccifer   (AP 41)

Sprawling growth with bright green leaves and stems with silvery white hairs. White flowers about 2 cms across. Petals deeply divided and seem to hang from the calyx. Fruit is a black shiny berry.

Height - 1 metre

THE PINK FAMILY Cont'd...

Night-flowering Catchfly

Silene noctiflora   (AP 40)

White flowers (sometimes tipped with pink) open at night. Flowers curled up during daylight. Bladders with prominent green veins. Whole plant very sticky and hairy.
Height - 40 cms

Sand Catchfly

Silene conica (AP 41)

Small pink flowers, less than 1 cm across. (the exception– in group 1) petals slightly notched. Bladder strongly marked with parallel veins.
Height - 30 cms

Sweet William

Dianthus barbatus (AP 42)

Petals occur in a variety of pinks and reds; they cluster to form a large (5 cms) flattened domed head.
Height - 30 cms

Deptford Pink

Dianthus armeria   (AP 42)

Dark, stiff, slender stem. Slightly downy. Flower heads with oval petals; pink and toothed along outer half. Flower heads about 1 cm across in loose clusters.
Height - 60 cms

THE PINK FAMILY Cont'd...

Cheddar Pink

Dianthus gratianopolitanus (AP 41)

Grows in mats with greyish leaves.
Height - 20 cms

Flowers pink and solitary,
about 1.5 cms across.

Group 2

The members of this group either have flowers with petals that are white or greenish-white or are without petals. Apart from Greater Stitchwort, Lesser Stitchwort and Field Mouse-ear, the flowers are small (1 cm or less). The main members of this group are Chickweeds, Stitchworts, Mouse-ears, Sandworts, Pearlworts and Spurreys.

Chickweeds These have pale green, oval, stalked leaves and weak sprawling stems. Typically they have 5 deeply divided petals (it can look as if they have ten narrow petals) and 5 sepals.

Water Chickweed

Myosoton aquaticum (AP 37)

Large bright green leaves, heart shaped at the base. Lower leaves have stalks. Straggly growth. White very deeply divided petals slightly longer than the sepals. Five styles and ten stamens.
Height - 1 metre

THE PINK FAMILY Cont'd...

Upright Chickweed   Moenchia erecta   (AP 37)

A rare species, limited mainly to the Minehead area. It is distinguished by being the only Chickweed with four individual petals.

Common Chickweed   Stellaria media   (AP 35)

Stems often dark-red with stalked lower leaves. Stems have a row of hairs along one side. The side with hairs alternates between the leaf joints. White flowers up to 10 mms across. Sepals have a thin white border. Stamens (3 to 8 in number) are reddish purple. *Height - 40 cms*

Lesser Chickweed   Stellaria pallida   (AP 35)

This is very like Common Chickweed but the flowers are smaller (5 mms across) and there are only one to three dull purple stamens.

Greater Chickweed   Stellaria neglecta   (AP 35)

White flowers about 9 to10 mms cross. *Height - 25 cms*

Has rows of hairs on the stems.

Has 10 dark-reddish stamens.

THE PINK FAMILY Cont'd...

Stitchworts

The leaves are without stalks, narrower and less bright green than those of the Chickweeds.

<u>**Greater Stitchwort**</u>   <u>**Stellaria holostea**</u> **(AP 36)**

Flowers are white and about 20 mms across. Petals are divided to about halfway down their length; they are twice as long as the sepals. Has square stem and the leaf edges are rough when stroked downwards.
Height - 60 cms

<u>**Lesser Stitchwort**</u>   <u>**Stellaria graminea**</u> **(AP 36)**

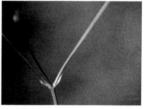

White petals are divided for most of their length. Flowers are about 10 mms across. Has a smooth stem and leaves with smooth edges. *Height - 30 cms*

<u>**Marsh Stitchwort**</u>   <u>**Stellaria palustris**</u> **(AP 36)**

White petals are divided for most of their length. Flowers are about 10 mms across. Sepals have a white edge. Stamens dark. *Height - 30 cms*

THE PINK FAMILY Cont'd...

Bog Stitchwort   Stellaria uliginosa   (AP 36)

Flowers small (6 mms across). Divided petals are shorter than the sepals. Leaves oval.
Height - 30 cms

Mouse-ears

Similar to Chickweeds but hairier and often sticky. Flowers white with five (except Sea Mouse-ear) deeply notched petals.

Sea Mouse-ear   Cerastium diffusum   (AP 37)

White petals shorter than the sepals. Flower parts usually in fours (not fives). Densely glandular.
Height - 20 cms

Snow-in-summer   Cerastium tomentosum   (AP 36)

Usually a garden escape.
The entire plant is a silvery white.
Height - 20 cms

Common Mouse-ear   Cerastium fontanum   (AP 37)

White flowers; sepals and petals about the same length. Sepals do not have a pale border.
Height - 40 cms

THE PINK FAMILY Cont'd...

Sticky Mouse-ear   Cerastium glomeratum (AP 37)

Compact head of white
flowers. Sepals and petals
are the same length.
Sepals when open have
a narrow pale border.
Stickily hairy.
Height - 40 cms

Dwarf Mouse-ear   Cerastium pumilum (AP 37)

Sepals and white petals are same length.
Sepals have a broad pale border.
Height - 10 cms

Little Mouse-ear   Cerastium semidecandrum (AP 37)

White petals shorter than the sepals.
Flowers carried in a compact head.
Very hairy and sticky.
Height - 15 cms

Sandworts

A difficult group. The flowers are white or greenish/white and the petals are not notched.

Sea Sandwort   Honckenya peploides (AP 35)

Flower greenish white and about 8 mm across. Compact growth form.
The only pearlwort with fleshy, almost triangular leaves, set closely together.
Height - 30 cms

THE PINK FAMILY Cont'd...

Three-nerved Sandwort

Moehringia trinervia (AP 35)

Leaves oval with three or more veins.
Green and about 2 cms long.
Petals are shorter than the sepals;
flowers about 6 mms across.
Height - sprawling to 40 cms

Spring Sandwort

Minuartia verna (AP 35)

Long slender stalks. Leaves narrow and
small. *Height - 15 cms*

Petals and sepals about the same length.

Thyme-leaved Sandwort

Arenaria serpyllifolia (AP 34)

Leaves greyish-green, unstalked
and oval each with one vein.
Sepals about twice as long as the petals.
Flowers about 7 mm across.
Anthers noticeably yellow.
Height - 30 cms

Slender Sandwort

Arenaria serpyllifolia (AP 34)

Similar to Thyme-leaved but smaller flowers (about 4 mm across). This is considered to
be a sub species (a very close relative) of Thyme Leaved Sandwort, hence they have the
same species title. *Height - 25 cms*

THE PINK FAMILY Cont'd...

Corn Spurrey   Spergula arvensis (AP 39)

The only Spurrey commonly found inland. A scattered arable weed, usually on the acid soils in West Somerset. Flowers pale pink about 6 mms across. Petal not notched and slightly longer than the sepals. Whole plant has sticky hairs.

Greater Sea-spurrey   Spergularia media (AP 39)

Leaves bright green, fleshy and hairless. Flowers about 10 mm across, petals slightly longer than the sepals. Has 5 long outer stamen and 5 short inner stamens.
Height - 20 cms

Lesser Sea-spurrey   Spergularia marina (AP 39)

Upper leaf surface has sticky hairs. Flowers about 7 mm across and petals often tipped purple. Petals shorter than the sepals.
Height - 20 cms

Sand Spurrey   Spergularia rubra (AP 39)

 Flowers about 4 mm across and pale pink. Petals shorter than the sepals. Can occur a little distance away from the immediate coast.
Height - 20 cms

THE PINK FAMILY Cont'd...

Pearlworts

Small, (the tallest species reach only about 15 cms), narrow leaved plants. Flowers with four or five white petals which are often very short lived, only the sepals persisting.

Knotted Pearlwort

Stem has knotted feel.
Height - 15 cms

Heath Pearlwort

Mat forming. Flowering stems are sticky and hairy; they project above the mat.
Height - 10 cms

Procumbent Pearlwort

Sagina nodosa (AP 38)

Flower has five white petals; petals longer than the sepals.

Sagina subulata (AP 38)

Flowers have five petals about the same length as the sepals.

Sagina procumbens (AP 38)

Forms a moss-like patch with creeping stems growing outwards. Flower stems grow from these outer shoots. Flowers have four very short-lived petals; four green, blunt sepals remain. *Height - 4 cms*

THE PINK FAMILY Cont'd...

Two more Pearlworts may be found.

Annual Pearlwort   **Sagina apetala (AP 38)**

Very similar to Procumbent Pearlwort but without a central leaf rosette.

Sea Pearlwort   **Sagina maritima (AP 38)**

A rare plant. In Somerset it is limited to the coast. Very similar to Procumbent Pearl-wort but has blunt fleshy leaves. Flowers usually without petals.

THE DOCK FAMILY   POLYGONACEAE

Herbaceous plants whose flowers have no petals, instead they have 3 - 6 sepals.
They have a papery wrapping round the stem at leaf junctions. Apart from Docks and Sorrels, the Family also includes Knotweeds, Knotgrass, Bistorts and Persicarias.

Docks and Sorrels

The very small and short lived flowers are carried in clusters on terminal spikes.
Leaves alternate up the stem.
The seed cases, which are important in identification, are very small, three-sided and with projecting ridges or valves.
The group readily hybridises.

THE DOCK FAMILY Cont'd....

Water Dock   Rumex hydrolapathum (AP 45)

Much the largest – up to 2 metres. Lower leaves can be up to 1 metre long. Grows near water.
Height - 2 metres

Seed-case wings are roundish and without teeth.

Curled Dock   Rumex crispus (AP 46)

Leaf curled along the outer edge.
Height - 1 metre

The seed-case has a broad outer wing which narrows to a point at the tip.

Clustered Dock   Rumex conglomeratus (AP 46)

Stem is often zig-zag shape. Whole plant looks 'straggly'. Leaves occur up amongst the flowering stem. Wings of the seed-case are extended downwards.

Height - 1 metre

THE DOCK FAMILY Cont'd....

Wood Dock

Similar to Clustered Dock but with very few, if any, leaves at the top of the stem.
Height - 1 metre

Rumex sanguineus (AP 47)

Seed-case is a broad oval without teeth.

Fiddle Dock

Rumex pulcher (AP 48)

The only dock with narrow, waisted (fiddle shaped) leaves. Low, spreading and with side branches at a wide angle to the main stem. Seed case is roughly triangular with numerous long teeth.
Height - 59 cms

Broad-leaved Dock

A stout plant with large leaves.
Height - 1 metre

Rumex obtusifolius (AP 48)

Seed-case broad with long spiky teeth, looks almost like a beetle.

Leaves heart shaped at base.

THE DOCK FAMILY Cont'd....

Golden Dock

Rumex maritimus (AP 48)

Golden yellow when mature. Seed cases close together give the plant a "fluffy" appearance. *Height - 50 cms*

Small seed-cases with long teeth.

Marsh Dock

Rumex palustris (AP 48)

Seed cases like Golden Dock, except the spines are slightly thicker. *Height - 70 cms*

Leaves long and thin. Plant turns orange/brown as it matures.

Sorrels

There are two Sorrels, each with long leaves with two lobes at the base. They are smaller and more delicate than the Docks. Other Sorrels, eg Wood Sorrel, are not related.

Common Sorrel

Rumex acetosa (AP 45)

Seed cases reddish with large flat, untoothed wings. Leaves arrow-shaped at the base, almost clasping the stem. *Height - 70 cms*

Sheep's Sorrel

Rumex acetosella   (AP 45)

Smaller than the Common Sorrel. Leaves with basal lobes which point outwards.
Height - 30 cms

Knotgrasses

Flowers are very small, white or pink, spaced along the stem. No distinction between the petals and sepals, together there are 5 of them. White/silver sheath at the base of the leaves.

Knotgrass

Polygonum aviculare   (AP 44)

Usually prostrate and spreading. Leaves on the main stems are larger than those on the side branches.
Height - 5 cms

Equal-leaved Knotgrass

Polygonum arenastrum   (AP 44)

Forms a very dense grey-green mat. Leaves on the main stems are the same size as those on the side branches. *Height - 5 cms*

THE DOCK FAMILY Cont'd....

Bistorts or Persicarias

Flowers in club-shaped heads, (apart from Water pepper). Petals pink, white or green/ white.

Amphibious Bistort   <u>Persicaria amphibia</u> **(AP 43)**

Usually growing in shallow water, this form has floating leaves. Can occur on wet ground; this form has an upright stem and hairy leaves. Flowers bright pink in a compact head.

Water-pepper   <u>Persicaria hydropiper</u> **(AP 43)**

More like a
Knotgrass
with small
pale pink-white
flowers. Leaves
long and
narrow. Has
a very strong
peppery
'after-taste'.

*Height of aquatic form 20 cms;
land form 50 cms. Height - 70 cms*

Tasteless Water-pepper   <u>Persicaria laxiflora</u> **(AP 43)**

Like the above but without the peppery taste.
Leaves long and narrow.
Flowers' heads may bend but they do not droop.
Height - 40 cms

THE DOCK FAMILY Cont'd....

Bistorts and Persicarias Cont'd....

Redshank (Redleg)

Persicaria maculosa   (AP 43)

Flowers pink and in a noticeable head. Stems go reddish with age and are swollen at the joints. Leaves have dark patch near their centre. *Height - 70cms*

Pale Persicaria

Persicaria lapathifolia   (AP 43)

Leaves up to 20mms wide. Stems green and sometimes downy. Leaves rarely have dark marking. Like Redshank but heads even more compact and green/white.
Height - 1 metre

Common Bistort

Persicaria bistorta   (AP 42)

Patch forming. Upper leaves oval and usually without a stalk. Lower leaves long and thin and without the marks present on Redshank leaves. Flowers pink and in a noticeable head. *Height - 1 metre*

THE DOCK FAMILY Cont'd....

Red Bistort

Flowers deep red.
Height - 1 metre

Persicaria amplexicaulis   (AP 42)

Leaves oval with a long slender tip.

Russian-vine

Rampant climber. Flowers prolifically, the
flower trusses can cover the whole plant.

Fallopia baldschuanica   (AP 45)

Leaves heart-shaped.
Height - 6 metres

Lesser Knotweed

Pink flowers, more open and
bell-shaped. *Height - 1 metres*

Persicaria campanulata   (AP 42)

Leaves long (15 cms) and narrow;
rounded at the base. Leaves downy on
the underside.

THE DOCK FAMILY Cont'd....

Japanese Knotweed   Fallopia japonica   (AP 44)

Flowers in hanging trusses along the stem. Leaves heart-shaped. Stems reddish with slightly zigzag growth. Forms bamboo like clumps. This is now regarded as an unwelcome plant and it should be eradicated. *Height 1.5 metres*

Himalayan Knotweed   Persicaria wallichii   (AP 42)

A scarce introduction. Very like Japanese Knotweed but the leaves are narrower and red veined.

Giant Knotweed   Fallopia sachalinensis   (AP 44)

Very tall (to 3 metres). Leaves larger and more triangular towards the tip than Japanese Knotweed. Flowers in long upright tapering spires. *Height 3 metres*

Black Bindweed   Fallopia convolvulus   (AP 45)

Weak sprawling climber. Winds clockwise around support. Flowers small, in loose spikes. Stems ridged and often red, leaves heart-shaped. Fruit is a small black dry nut. Not related to other Bindweeds. *Height 1 metre*

THE SEA LAVENDER FAMILY   PLUMBAGINACEAE

The wild members of this family are coastal plants.

Common Sea-lavender   Limonium vulgare   (AP 48)

Usually in large drifts on coastal salt marsh. Flower stalks branch only in the upper half, stems are round. Green leaflet at the base of the flower branches.
Height - 40 cms

Rock Sea-lavender   Limonium binervosum   (AP 49)

Usually on cliff ledges etc… Flower stem branches below half way.
Height - 30 cms

Winged leaf stalks. Red leaflet at base of flower branches.

Thrift   Armeria maritima   (AP 49)

Tight cushions of dark green, grass-like leaves.
Height - 30 cms

Flowers on distinct heads standing well clear of the leaves.

Brown petal-like papery bracts below the flower heads.

THE PAEONY FAMILY   PAEONIACEAE

Sometimes written as Peony. The only member is often called the Steep Holm Paeony.

Paeony   Paeonia officinalis (AP 49)

Large (10 cm diameter) pink flowers on single stems. Ten petals forming a cup.
Leaves in 3 lobes. Seed pods have a dense cover of hairs. *Height - 80 cms*

THE ST JOHN'S-WORT FAMILY   CLUSIACEAE

Apart from their size, the flowers of the members of
this family are similar. They each have five yellow petals
arranged in an open cup shape; numerous stamens and
three central styles. The petals and sepals have various
patterns of black dots and/or translucent spaces.

Rose-of-Sharon   Hypericum calycinum (AP 49)

Has the largest flowers, 6-8 cms across. Stems are reddish, oval in section
with four very faint ridges. Leaves in pairs along the stem. *Height - 40 cms*

Tutsan   Hypericum androsaemum (AP 49)

 Shrubby with large leaves in
pairs. (8cms long and 4 cms
wide). Flowers up to 3 cms
across. Stem reddish with
two ridges of hair. On any
one flower head one sepal
is shorter than the rest.
Fruits are red/black berries.

Height - 70 cms

THE ST JOHN'S-WORT FAMILY Cont'd...

Marsh St John's-wort   Hypericum elodes (AP 51)

Low growing (25 cms) with closely packed downy grey/green leaves. Grows in shallow
water in acid conditions. Flowers rarely open fully; petals fringed with red dots.
Height - 25 cms

Square-stalked St John's-wort   Hypericum tetrapterum (AP 50)

Usually grows in a wet/damp habitat. Stem square with ridges at each corner. Sepals
narrow pointed and with no or very few black dots. *Height - 1 metre*

Imperforated St John's-wort   Hypericum maculatum (AP 50)

Stem square but without ridges. Petals have black markings.
No translucent dots on the leaves. Sepals blunt. *Height - 80 cms*

THE ST JOHN'S-WORT FAMILY Cont'd...

Perforate St John's-wort   Hypericum perforatum (AP 50)

Flowers about 2 cms across. *Height - 80 cms*

Leaves have translucent dots.

Petals have black dots on their edges.

Hairy St John's-wort   Hypericum hirsutum (AP 50)

Flower pale yellow in loose spike.
Leaves have translucent dots.
Sepals pointed with black dots on the
margin. Has downy/hairy round stem.
Height - 1 metre

Pale St John's-wort   Hypericum montanum (AP 51)

Fewer flowers. *Height - 1 metre*

Sepals edged with very small black dots.

Stems round and hairless. Black dots on the under edges of leaves; no translucent dots.

THE ST JOHN'S-WORT FAMILY Cont'd...

Slender St John's-wort

Hypericum pulchrum (AP 50)

Stem smooth and round; plant slim. Petals and sepals have black and red spots. Petals red on the underside. Leaves have translucent spots. *Height - 60 cms*

Trailing St John's-wort

Hypericum humifusum (AP 50)

Has prostrate or creeping habit. Stem has two ridges. Petals tend to be narrower, giving a star-shaped appearance. Petals are pale yellow and have black dots, the sepals also have black dots. *Height - 25 cms*

THE LIME TREE FAMILY   TILIACEAE

These are all tall trees with distinctive fruits.

Lime   Tilia x vulgaris (AP 51)

Although this is a hybrid, it is frequently planted and is now treated as part of our natural flora. Winter twigs have deep chestnut coloured buds which occur at the tips of short side branches. The trunk is

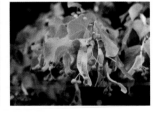

greyish with vertical cracks. The leaves are oval and toothed, 'lop-sided' at the base and about 8cms long; they end in a distinct point. The nutlets hang in small clusters from wings. The trunk is often surrounded by sucker growth. *Height - 40 metres*

THE LIME TREE FAMILY Cont'd….

Large-leaved Lime

Leaves 10-12 cms long and have a pointed tip. Not lop-sided. Trunk is greyish and with few cracks.

Tilia platyphyllos (AP 51)

Nutlets are downy and with about 6 in each cluster.
Height - 40 metres

Small-leaved Lime

Leaves about 5cms long, are rounded, only slightly 'lop-sided' and with a distinctive pointed tip.

Tilia cordata (AP 51)

Leaf has rust coloured down on the underside near the leaf stalk.
Height - 30 metres

THE MALLOW FAMILY

MALVACEAE

Usually five large slightly notched petals. Most species have pink/purple petals. Has a double row of sepals.

THE MALLOW FAMILY Cont'd...

Hollyhock

Garden escape. Tall (3 metres) spire of flowers; petal colour varies – red, pinks and yellow.

Alcea rosea (AP 53)

Height - 3 metres

Tree-mallow

Shrub-like growth. Leaves woolly and ivy-shaped. Flowers in clusters; purple with dark centre, sepals form a cup.

Lavatera arborea   (AP 52)

Height - 2 metres

Marsh-mallow

Althaea officinalis   (AP 53)

Flowers pale almost white, 4 cms across, centre dark purple. Edge of petals only slightly wavy. Leaves downy, ivy-shaped and toothed.
Height - 1.5 metres

THE MALLOW FAMILY Cont'd...

Musk-mallow   Malva moschata   (AP 52)

Flowers pale pink, petals notched.
Height - 80 cms

Leaves much divided.

Dwarf Mallow   Malva neglecta   (AP 52)

Sprawling growth.
Flowers pale pink/white
about 2.5 cm across.
Leaves vary from
five lobed, to sometimes
rounded and heart
shaped.

Height - 25 cms

Common Mallow   Malva sylvestris   (AP 52)

Much branched and often
sprawling. Petals purple
with dark veins, petals
notched. Flower about
4 cms across, and much
longer than the sepals.
Leaves usually 5 lobed.

Height - 1 metre

Royal Mallow   Lavatera trimestris   (AP 53)

Rose pink flowers about 5
cms across. Small dark
centre to the flower, petals
wavy edged, not notched.

Height - 1 metre

THE SUNDEW FAMILY   DROSERACEAE

Small, (10 to 15 cms) insectivorous plants. Rosette of leaves with reddish glandular hairs which secrete a sticky gum, 'the dew'. It is this gum that traps insects.

Round-leaved Sundew   Drosera rotundifolia (AP 53)

Round leaves, about 1 cm across form a basal rosette. White flowers are on a 10 cms stem which rises out of the centre of rosette.
Height - 15 cms

Flower spike is curved when young, straightening as it matures.

Oblong-leaved Sundew   Drosera intermedia (AP 54)

Leaves are narrow and oblong, tapering to the leaf stalk. *Height - 7 cms*

Flower stalk is short, not much longer than the leaves.

THE ROCK ROSE FAMILY   CISTACEAE

Low growing plants with downy, thickened oval leaves. Flowers have 5 petals, numerous stamens, 2 inner and 3 outer sepals. Usually growing on hillsides.

Common Rock-rose   Helianthemum nummularium (AP 54)

Flowers bright yellow, 2.5 cms across. Leaves long narrow, downy on the underside. Margins are in-rolled.

Height - 25 cms

THE ROCK ROSE FAMILY Cont'd....

White Rock-rose

Helianthemum apenninum (AP 54)

Flowers white and leaves downy-white on both surfaces. Brean Down is the only "wild" site for this plant; there it is common on the South side. *Height - 15 cms*

THE VIOLET AND PANSY FAMILY   VIOLACEAE

Flowers with five petals, the bottom one carried back to form a spur. They have five leafy sepals which remain after the petals have fallen and enclose the seed pod. In general Violets have a broad flower face whilst pansies have a longer one.

Wild Pansy

Viola tricolor (AP 56)

Flowers small (1.5 cms). Usually the lower petals are creamy yellow and the upper ones purple. Sepals especially the upper ones, shorter than the petals. Dune form often has more yellow on the petals. *Height - 40 cms but straggly.*

Mountain Pansy

Viola lutea (AP 56)

Usually yellow, lower petal especially may have dark markings. Flowers 2.5 cms across and on long stalks; lower petal comes to a point. Leaves, almost hairless, are a long oval shape.

Height - 20 cms

A colour variant.

THE VIOLET AND PANSY FAMILY Cont'd...

Field Pansy   Viola arvensis   (AP 56)

Flowers small (1.5 cms) and lower petal often has a distinct 'chin'. Petals are creamy white and slightly shorter than the sepals. *Height - 25 cms*

Marsh Violet   Viola palustris   (AP 55)

Has rounded kidney shaped leaves. Flowers about 1.5 cms across, pale violet with darker veins. Spur pale and blunt. Stipules either smooth or with very small teeth. Has runners. *Height - 25 cms*

Sweet Violet   Viola odorata   (AP 54)

Leaves downy and heart shaped. Plant has runners. *Height - 15 cms*

Flowers 1.5 cms across. Violet (or white) and scented.

Stipules pointed and fringed.

THE VIOLET AND PANSY FAMILY Cont'd...

Hairy Violet   Viola hirta (AP 54)

Flowers like Sweet Violet
but without scent.
Stems covered in spread-
ing hairs. No runners.

Height - 15 cms

Common Dog-violet   Viola riviniana (AP 55)

Forms clumps with non-
flowering centres. Leaves
are heart shaped and
toothed. Flowering shoots
are on edge of rosette.
Flowers 2 cms across. Deep
purple lines on the petals.
Spur blunt and pale with
groove at the tip.

Height - 10 cms

Early Dog-violet   Viola reichenbachiana (AP 55)

Very similar to Common
Dog-violet, but flowers
are paler and the spur is
without a groove and
darker than the petals.

Height - 10 cms

Heath Dog-violet   Viola canina (AP 55)

Leaves oval and toothed.
Heart-shaped at the base.
Flowers 15 mm across
and with a white/yellow/
greenish spur. The spur
is straight and blunt.

Height - 10 cms

THE VIOLET AND PANSY FAMILY Cont'd...

Pale Dog-violet   Viola lactea   (AP 55)

Similar to Heath Dog-violet but the leaves are without the heart-shaped base.
Flowers pale and spur greenish. *Height - 20 cms*

THE TAMARISK FAMILY   TAMARICACEAE

There is only one member of this family referred to in the *Atlas*; the very distinctive bush.

Tamarisk   Tamarix gallica   (AP 56)

Leaves mid-green, light and feathery. Flowers in pink trusses. *Height - 3 metres*

THE GOURD FAMILY   CUCURBITACEAE

Most members of this family tend to occur as casuals and can be thought of as garden
escapes, eg Melons, Marrows and Pumpkins.

White Bryony   Bryonia dioica (AP 56)

A climber which uses its spiralling and tightening tendrils to pull itself up. Half the
tendrils spiral clockwise whilst the other half is anticlockwise. Flowers about 1.5 cms
across have five white creamy petals. Leaves are fig-like. Fruit is a red berry.
Height - climbing to 3-4 metres

THE WILLOW FAMILY   SALICACEAE

A family of trees or shrubs. Typically, Willows have long thin leaves whilst the shrubs, commonly called Sallows, have round/oval leaves. Both these groups have catkins which grow upwards, (or outwards), whilst the third member, Poplars, have pendant catkins. The seeds of all of them have long silky hairs and, unfortunately, they frequently hybridise. The male and female flowers are on separate trees. 'Pussy' catkins are only on the male flowers especially of sallows. In winter, each bud has a single scale which covers the whole bud.

Creeping Willow   Salix repens (AP 61)

A very low growing
(one metre but often less
than 30 cms) shrub.
It has a creeping rootstock.
Leaves oval.
Height - 1 metre

Crack-willow   Salix fragilis (AP 58)

Tall, spreading tree.
Twigs snap easily.
Long thin, slightly toothed
leaves, unequal at the tip.
Usually by water and
often pollarded.
Height - 2.5 metres

Large catkins.

Seeds with "parachute"
hairs.

THE WILLOW FAMILY Cont'd......

White-willow   Salix alba   (AP 58)

Leaves long (8 cms), thin and covered in silky white hairs.
Height - 25 metres

Symmetrical at the top of the leaf, but sometimes bending to one side.
Twigs pliable.

Osier (Withy)   Salix viminalis   (AP 59)

Stems (from root stock) are long, straight and flexible and used in basket making. Leaves long (15 cms) and narrow with white hairs on the underside. Leaf edge wavy and in-rolled when young. *Height - 8 metres*

Goat Willow (Great Sallow)   Salix caprea   (AP 60)

Leaves oval and soft to the touch.
Height - 5 metres

Catkins silvery white, opening to yellow. The plant is often called Pussy Willow.

89

THE WILLOW FAMILY Cont'd......

Grey Willow (Sallow)/Rusty Willow   Salix cinerea (AP 60)

Two closely related sub species. Leaves oval, toothed in the upper half. Leaf margins often in-rolled. Toothed stipules. A sub-species has red hairs on the underside of the leaf. *Height - 7 metres*

Eared Willow   Salix aurita (AP 61)

Small shrub, 2 metres.
Leaves oval and often wrinkled.
A pair of ear-shaped stipules at the base of the leaf stalk. Side branches grow at right-angles to main stem, giving it a distinctly bushy appearance.
Height - 2 metres

Almond Willow   Salix triandra (AP 59)

Another species, but less common, with ear-shaped stipules. The leaves are toothed and lance-shaped, (8cms long). A much taller (8 metres) species and more tree like.

Aspen   Populus tremula (AP 57)

Leaf stalk flattened. Leaves round and wavy edged; hairy when young.
Height - 20 metres

Trunk frequently surrounded by suckers. Bark grey with horizontal cracks.

White Poplar   Populus alba (AP 57)

Leaf ivy-shaped, dark green above and white below. Buds and young shoots are downy white. Trunk is pale grey with bands of dark diamond shaped cracks. Frequently has suckers. *Height - 20 metres*

Black Poplar   Populus nigra (AP 57)

Leaves without white down,
triangular and finely toothed.
Height - 25 metres

Bark is grey with boles. Later it develops wavy ridges. Rarely has suckers.

Lombardy-poplar   Populus nigra (AP 58)

A form of the Black Poplar. Tall columnar trees.
Branches grow upwards and close to the trunk.
Leaves toothed, wide with a pointed tip.
Height - 30 metres

THE CABBAGE (CRUCIFER) FAMILY   BRASSICACEAE (CRUCIFERAE)

The name Crucifer refers to the fact the the petals and sepals of the members of this group form a distinct cross. Usually they also have six stamens and two carpels.
To identify the species, not only the flowers but the pods, the leaves of any basal rosette and the stem are all significant.

The common names can be misleading in that many cresses eg. Bittercress, Rock-cress, Winter-cress, Water-cress and Swine-cress all belong to different groups within the Family. In contrast, Garlic Mustard and Wallflower are in the same group.

To aid identification it is possible to divide the Family into smaller groups depending on flower colour and pod shape.

Group 1 Those plants whose flowers are in the pink-purple range; (garden escapes may show a wide degree of colour variation and this should be allowed for). Pods round or oval.

Honesty   Lunaria annua   (AP 66)

Flowers are magenta, or occasionally white. Pods disc-shaped. The two outer walls break away leaving a silver central wall. This makes it very popular in dried flower arrangements. *Height - 1 metre*

Aubretia   Aubrieta deltoidea   (AP 65)

Low growing 'rockery' plant. Flowers pink to purple. Leaves greyish and thick. Pods are oval with a long 'beak', total length 15 mms. *Height - 10 cms*

THE CABBAGE FAMILY Cont'd....

Garden Candytuft

Iberis umbellata   (AP 68)

Flowers form a tight umbrella-shaped head. Petal colour varies from white to pink to purple. Outer pair of petals are bigger than the inner pair. Pods are oval , grooved at the top and with a central 'beak'. *Height - 20 cms*

Sea Rocket

Cakile maritima   (AP 71)

Flowers pink, (sometimes white), 15 mms across. Leaves grey-green, fleshy and pinnate. A coastal species. Pods oval. *Height - 50 cms*

Group 2 Flowers pink or purple. Pods long.

Dame's-violet

Hesperis matronalis   (AP 62)

Flowers deep pink or white, about 2 cms across. Individual flowers close together making a flower head. Leaves long, narrow and toothed. Pods long (10 cms) narrow and curving.

Height - 80 cms

93

THE CABBAGE FAMILY Cont'd....

Night-scented Stock

Matthiola longipetala   (AP 63)

Flowers pale puple, about 5mms across. Long and thin petals which curl up in sunlight. *Height - 40 cms*

Pod long and thin with two 'horns' at the end.

Cuckooflower

Cardamine pratensis   (AP 64)

Also called Milkmaids and Lady's smock. Flower pale pink about 15 mms across. Basal rosette of much divided leaves, stem leaves much reduced. Pods long and thin. *Height - 60 cms*

THE CABBAGE FAMILY Cont'd....

Group 3 Yellow flowers with round or oval pods.

Golden Alison   **Alyssum saxatile (AP 66)**

Leaves long, thin and grey-green. Leaves slightly in-rolled along their length.

Flowers in a bright yellow truss; individual flowers about 6 mm across.
Height - 30 cms

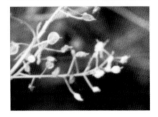

Pods almost round; outer cases soon fall off leaving transparent central wall.

Marsh Yellow-cress   **Rorippa palustris (AP 64)**

Becoming common but often difficult to get near since it grows on muddy ditch/stream banks. Flowers about 3 mms across with sepals as long as the petals. Leaves long and toothed; base of leaf stalk forks back around the stem. Pods short, dumpy, oval with a short beak. *Height - 30 cms*

Group 4 Yellow flowers with long thin pods.

Flixweed   **Descurainia sophia (AP 62)**

Yellow flowers 4 mms across. Pod long without any beak. Much divided leaves producing a 'spiky' look.
Height - 1 metre

95

Hedge Mustard   Sisymbrium officinale   (AP 61)

Flowers yellow and about 3 mms across. Pods about 15 mms long and without a 'beak'. Stem-leaves and pods pressed close to the stem or side branch giving a 'rigid' appearance to the plant. Ground rosette of leaves; often difficult to find amongst neighbouring plants.
Height - 70 cms

Wallflower   Erysimum cheiri   (AP 62)

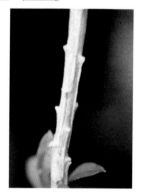

Petals commonly yellow but with occasional patches of red. Sepals half the length of the petals; flower about 15 mms across. Stem has ridges. Pods, about 3 cms, do not overtop the flowers.
Height - 60 cms

Black Mustard   Brassica nigra   (AP 71)

Flower about 15 mms across. All leaves with stalks, upper leaves lanceolate, lower leaves deeply lobed. Pods with a short beak, held close to stem.
Height - 2 metres

THE CABBAGE FAMILY Cont'd....

Hoary Mustard   Hirschfeldia incana   (AP 71)

A rare introduction. Like Black Mustard but leaves with up to nine pairs of leaflets.
Coarse white hairs, especially on the lower leaves.
Height - 1.2 metres

Wild Radish   Raphanus raphanistrum   (AP 72)

Flowers variable yellow or white, usually
with purple veins. Leaves with large end-
lobe. Pods beaded with a slender 'beak'.
Height - 75 cms

Sea Radish   Raphanus raphanistrum   (AP 72)

Sometimes this is considered a variation of the Wild
Radish but the leaf so divided as to be almost pinnate.
Pods extremely beaded. Usually 3 or 4 seeds in the pod.
Height - 1.5 metres

THE CABBAGE FAMILY Cont'd....

White Mustard   Sinapis alba   (AP 71)

Flowers pale yellow.
Upper leaves stalked and lobed.
Pod very beaded and with 'beak'
as long as the pod.
Height - 80 cms

Charlock   Sinapis arvensis   (AP 71)

Flowers, 20 mms across, strong yellow. Upper leaves lobed
but without stalks. Pods beaded and with a short tapering
'beak'. *Height - 70 cms*

Rape (Oil-seed Rape)   Brassica napus   (AP 70)

Flowers, 25 mms across, vivid yellow. Upper leaves have wavy
edge and clasp the stem. Flowers over-top the pods and the
buds over-top the flowers. Pods, 10 cms long are not beaded.
Height - 1.2 metres

THE CABBAGE FAMILY Cont'd....

Wild Turnip   Brassica rapa   (AP 70)

Similar to Rape but with smaller, 15 mms flowers. Usually on river banks. Long pod with longish beak. Flowers overtop the buds. *Height - 1 metre*

Treacle Mustard   Erysimum cheiranthoides   (AP 62)

Flowers about 8 mms across, petals twice as long as the sepals. Leaves long and toothed. Stems ridged. Pods about 2.5 cms long and do not over-top the flowers. *Height - 80 cms*

Eastern Rocket   Sisymbrium orientale   (AP 61)

Flowers about 7 mms across; petals nearly twice as long as the sepals. Basal leaves with spiky side lobes and a long end-lobe. Stem leaves stalked and more lanceolate. Pods long and over-topping the flowers. *Height - 80 cms*

THE CABBAGE FAMILY Cont'd….

Annual Wall-rocket

Diplotaxis muralis   (AP 70)

Flowers about 12 mms across..
Stem almost leafless.
Pods about 4 cms long.
Basal rosette of lobed slightly fleshy leaves.
Height - 60 cms

Perennial Wall-rocket

Diplotaxis tenuifolia   (AP 70)

A rare introduction. Very like Annual Wall-rocket. Basal leaves sharply toothed. Stem leaves present and lanceolate. Flowers 2 cms across, (larger than Annual Wall-rocket). Pod up to 6 cms. *Height - 80 cms*

Creeping Yellow-cress

Rorippa sylvestris (AP 64)

Flowers about 5 mms across; yellow petals longer than the sepals. Pods have long stalk. Leaves have narrow leaflets.

Height - 50 cms

THE CABBAGE FAMILY Cont'd....

Winter-cresses

Barbarea vulgaris   **(AP 63)**
Barbarea verna   **(AP 63)**

The second species is often called American Winter-cress.

Both species have flowers carried in clusters. The flowers each have four vivid yellow petals and measure about 8 mms across. The leaves are shiny and lobed.

In Winter-cress the end leaf lobe is large and the pod is straight with a tapering edge.

In American Winter-cress, the end leaf lobe is small and the pod is incurved.

Group 5   White flowers with long pods.

Garlic Mustard

Alliaria petiolata   **(AP 62)**

 Leaves bright green, heart-shaped and toothed. Flowers about 6 mms across. Petals about twice as long as sepals. Has garlic smell when crushed.

Height - 1 metre

Thale Cress   **Arabidopsis thaliana   (AP 62)**

Small (about 10 cms tall) thin looking   Pods (20 mms) straight but
plant. Flowers about 3 mms across.   projecting outwards.
Basal rosette of narrow oval hairy   *Height - 10 cms*
leaves. Few stem leaves.

Water-cress   **Rorippa nasturtium-aquaticum (AP 63)**

Grows floating in water. Stems hollow and hairless. Flowers (6 cms across) in dense
heads. Pods (15 mms) on a straight 10 mms stalk. Leaves with lobes; terminal lobe is
large. *Height - 20 cms above the water level.*

Narrow-fruited Water-cress   **Rorippa microphylla (AP 64)**

As Water-cress except for pod which is   Terminal leaf lobe is not noticeably
longer (2.0 cms) on a curved stalk.   longer.
Height - 20 cms

THE CABBAGE FAMILY Cont'd....

Bittercresses
Have much divided basal leaves which are usually stalked.

| **Hairy Bitter-cress** | **Cardamine hirsuta   (AP 65)** |

Not obviously hairy. In young plant leaves form a rosette. Later the stem lengthens and carries a few leaves. Flowers 3 mms across; 4 stamens. White petals soon lost. Pods 25 mms, overtopping the buds.

Height - 30 cms

| **Wavy Bitter-cress** | **Cardamine flexuosa   (AP 65)** |

Similar to Hairy Bitter-cress. Stem has several pinnate leaves; leaflets are toothed. Stem bends at the leaf joints. Flower has 6 stamens and the tips of the pods are level with the flowers.

Height - 40 cms

Rock-cresses
Hairy low growing plants with slightly fleshy leaves.

| **Hairy Rock-cress** | **Arabis hirsuta   (AP 65)** |

Basal rosette leaves hairy, oval and slightly toothed. Stem leaves untoothed and held close to the stem. Pods (35 mms) also held close to stem. Flowers, 4 mms across in small spray. *Height - 60 cms*

THE CABBAGE FAMILY Cont'd....

Garden Arabis   ### Arabis caucasica (AP 65)

Lower leaves with short stalks form greyish, hairy mat. Upper leaves toothed and clasping the stem. Pods held at an angle about 35 mms long.
Height - 30 cms

Group 6 Plants with white flowers and round/oval pods.

Shepherd's-purse   ### Capsella bursa-pastoris (AP 68)

Lower leaves variable, upper leaves toothed and grasping the stem. Flowers 2-3 mms across, petals twice as long as sepals. Distinctive heart-shaped pods.
Height - 30 cms

THE CABBAGE FAMILY Cont'd....

Common Whitlow-grass   **Erophila verna (AP 66)**

Flowers, 4 mms across, with deeply cleft petals. Leaves with few small lateral lobes, no stem leaves. Pods oval.
Height - 10 cms

Wall Whitlow-grass   **Draba muralis (AP 66)**

Flowers (3 mms) slightly smaller than Common Whitlow grass. Has few leaves which clasp the stem and basal rosette of lobed leaves. Pods oval on stalks as long as the pods.

Sweet Alison   **Lobularia maritima (AP 66)**

Grows in compact clumps. Flowers, 6 mms across, sometimes pinkish.
Height - 20 cms

Leaves narrow, unstalked and untoothed. Pods egg shaped.

THE CABBAGE FAMILY Cont'd....

The Scurvy grasses are not grasses. The first three typically grow on coastal mud areas.

Common Scurvygrass   **Cochlearia officinalis (AP 67)**

Flowers, sometimes pinkish in a globular head. Basal leaves rounded or kidney-shaped. Stem leaves more oblong, stalked and toothed. *Height - 50 cms*

English Scurvygrass   **Cochlearia anglica (AP 67)**

Flowers up to 12 mms across. Lower leaves oblong with narrow base. Upper leaves clasp the stem. Pods flattened. *Height - 40 cms*

Danish Scurvygrass   **Cochlearia danica (AP 67)**

Stem often prostrate. Flowers, 5 mms across, sometimes with pink tinge. Basal leaves have longer stalk. Stem leaves heart or ivy-shaped. Pods egg-shaped. *Height - 15 cms*

THE CABBAGE FAMILY Cont'd....

Alpine Scurvygrass   Cochlearia pyrenaica (AP 67)

Prostrate growth and not limited to the coastal region. Flowers 6 mms across. Basal leaves small, less than 2 mms. Stem leaves ivy-shaped and clasping the stem. Pods egg-shaped, pod slightly shorter than its stalk.
Height - 30 cms

Pennycresses

Seed pod has a notch at the top and the stem leaves, unstalked, clasp at the stem.

Alpine Penny-cress   Thlaspi caerulescens (AP 68)

Anthers are violet in flowers about 6 mms across. Leaves greyish. Pods heart-shaped with a long style; not obviously winged.
Height - 40 cms

Field Penny-cress   Thlaspi arvensis (AP 68)

Hairless and stinking when crushed. No basal rosette. Stem leaves long, sometimes toothed and clasping the stem with arrow-shaped bases. Flowers 5 mms across and with yellow anthers. Pods flat and winged, spoon-shaped when young.
Height - 50 cms

107

THE CABBAGE FAMILY Cont'd....

Candytufts Large showy flowers forming a compact 'umbrella' head, outer two petals of each individual flower are larger than the inner two.

Perennial Candytuft  **Iberis sempervirens (AP 68)**

Long, thin dark-green leaves. Sprawling growth. Pods round, notched and with short beaks. *Height - 30 cms*

Pepperworts Difficult to distinguish from Penny-cresses but pods of pepperworts have two upwards pointing wings.

Garden Cress  **Lepidium sativum (AP 68)**

A Pepperwort, despite the name. It is the cress of 'Mustard and Cress'. Upper leaves divided into three pointed lobed leaflets. Pods are heart-shaped with wings. *Height - 40 cms*

Field Pepperwort **Lepidium campestre (AP 69)**

The upper leaves are greyish and hairy. They clasp the stem and have two arrow-shaped lobes. *Height - 60 cms*

THE CABBAGE FAMILY Cont'd....

Smith's Pepperwort

Lepidium heterophyllum (AP 69)

Stem leaves clasp the stem with rounded lobes. Petals are white but the anthers are purple.

Pods similar to Field Pepperwort.
Height - 50 cms

Narrow-leaved Pepperwort

Lepidium ruderale (AP 69)

Stinks when crushed. Leaves long and thin. Flowers often without petals. Plant often sprawls. Pod wings are heart-shaped.
Height - 30 cms

Hoary Cress

Lepidium draba (AP 69)

Leaves hairless, coarsely toothed and clasping the stem. Large loose flower heads, individual flowers are about 5 mms across. Pods heart-shaped with a 'beak'.
Height - 90 cms

THE CABBAGE FAMILY Cont'd....

Swine-cresses Low growing prostrate plants with very small flowers.

Swine-cress   **Coronopus squamatus   (AP 69)**

Pinnate grey-green leaves with toothed leaflets. Flowers small on very short stalks,
(about 2 mms) in a compact head in the angle of the leaf. Pods fan-shaped with ridges.
Height - 20 cms

Lesser Swine-cress   **Coronopus didymus   (AP 70)**

Petal-less flowers on distinct stalk. Leaves much divided. Pods like two eggs side by side.
Height - 5 cms

Horse-radish   **Armoracia rusticana   (AP 64)**

Leaves, up to 40 cms, oval with curled edges. Flowers,
up to 10 mms across in trusses. Pods globular with
short 'beak'. A coarse large plant.
Height - 60 cms

THE WELD FAMILY   RESEDACEAE

At first sight, this family locally consists of two similarly tall upright plants, both with small yellow flowers. Their leaves however, are quite different.

Weld   **Reseda luteola (AP 72)**

Tall (1.5 metres) spire of yellow/ green flowers each with 4 petals. Leaves long and thin.

Height - 1.5 metres

Wild Mignonette   **Reseda lutea (AP 73)**

Medium height (75 cms) spire of yellow/green flowers, each with 6 petals. Leaves spiky and pinnate.
Height - 75 cms

THE CROWBERRY FAMILY   EMPETRACEAE

The only member of this family present is the Crowberry itself.

Crowberry   **Empetrum nigrum (AP 73)**

Mat forming evergreen. Flowers very small, almost stalk-less, at the base of the leaves. Leaves long and thin with inrolled edges and very close together. Young green fruit ripens to a black round berry.

Height - 1 metre

THE HEATH FAMILY   ERICACEAE

The members of this family are bushes or low-growing shrubs. They are associated with acid soils.

Rhododendron   **Rhododendron ponticum (AP 73)**

An evergreen shrub. Flowers large, pink-purple. On maturity the anthers and stigma protrude in front of the five petals. Leaves shiny dark green and oval. *Height - 5 metres*

Yellow Azalea   **Rhododendron luteum (AP 73)**

Similar to the Rhododendron but smaller with yellow flowers. Leaves oval but toothed. *Height - 2 metres*

Heather (Ling)   **Calluna vulgaris (AP 74)**

Has spikes of small, purple flowers. Leaves small and narrow, incurled, almost conifer-like. Plant of open moors. *Height - 60 cms*

THE HEATH FAMILY Cont'd...

Bell Heather

Erica cinerea (AP 74)

Flowers larger and brighter purple than Heather, (easily seen as bell-shaped).
Height - 60 cms

Leaves greener and longer and usually in threes.

Cross-leaved Heath

Erica tetralix (AP 74)

Leaves in fours, forming distinct series of crosses along the stem. Flowers pale pink/purple in clusters at the top of the stem. Usually in very wet ground.
Height - 60 cms

Bog-rosemary

Andromeda polifolia (AP 73)

Usually in or near wet acid bog, often with Sphagnum moss. Flowers pink on long stalks in a loose truss.

Leaves narrow elliptical, green above and white below.
Height - 30 cms

THE HEATH FAMILY Cont'd...

Checkerberry

Gaultheria procumbens (AP 74)

Very low growing (15 cms). Cream flowers in the angles of stem and leaf. Fruit a red berry. Oval leaves, finely toothed. *Height - 15 cms*

Bilberry (Whortleberry)

Vaccinium myrtillus (AP 75)

Deciduous shrub with mid-green leaves. Leaves finely toothed. Flowers pinkish, almost closed-bell shape. Fruit purple (and delicious!). *Height - 30 cms*

THE PRIMROSE FAMILY

PRIMULACEAE

All the members are herbaceous. The flowers have their petals etc in sets of five, with the petals usually fused at the base to form a tube.

Water-violet

Hottonia palustris (AP 76)

The only member that grows in water. Submerged, much-divided leaves. Flowers with pink petals are carried above the water surface in distinct whorls. It is not a violet; it gets its name from the pink/violet petals.

Height - stems about 25cms above the water surface.

THE PRIMROSE FAMILY Cont'd...

Primrose   **Primula vulgaris   (AP 75)**

Each flower has its own hairy stalk. Notched yellow petals, colour deepening towards the centre. Flower exists in two forms, pin and thrum, depending on the length of the style. Leaves are a wrinkled spoon-shape, tapering to the stalk, about 15 cms long. *Height - 15 cms*

Cowslip   **Primula veris   (AP 75)**

Flowers in a cluster on a downy stalk. Flowers usually hang downwards, exposing the ring of sepals. Flowers a deeper yellow than the Primrose. Leaves very like the primrose but smaller, less tapered about 10 cms long. *Height - 25 cms*

Japanese Cowslip   **Primula japonica   (AP 76)**

Grows very near water, eg bank of stream. Flowers can be red, yellow or white and carried in whorls. Many garden varieties, especially the yellow ones now grow wild. Leaves rounded oval with stalks. *Height - 50 cms*

THE PRIMROSE FAMILY Cont'd...

Yellow Loosestrife   Lysimachia vulgaris   (AP 76)

Tall, up to one metre. Flowers in terminal branched spray, flowers 2 cms.
Leaves slightly downy, oval with pointed tips. Sepals have reddish border.
Height - 1 metre

Dotted Loosestrife   Lysimachia punctata   (AP 77)

Flowers close to stem,
not in loose spray.
Grows as a clump of
upright stems. Leaves
and stem faintly downy.
Height - 80 cms

Yellow Pimpernel   Lysimachia nemorum   (AP 76)

Creeping growth form,
stems stretch 30 cms. Petals
rounder and more cup-
shaped; closer to the stem.
Leaves opposite in pairs but
more rounded than the
Pimpernel. Flowers larger
than the Pimpernel (20 mms).

Height - 10 cms

Creeping-Jenny   Lysimachia nummularia   (AP 76)

Creeping growth form, stems stretch 40
cms. Flowers like small (15 mms) yellow
stars. Flowers held above the stem on
slender stalks. Leaves opposite
in pairs, oval with pointed tips.
Height - 10 cms

THE PRIMROSE FAMILY Cont'd...

Scarlet Pimpernel

Anagallis arvensis (AP 77)

Prostrate annual with a
square stem. Flowers with
long stalks and deep red
petals, darkening towards
the centre. Leaves stalk-
less, oval with pointed tips.
Height - 25 cms

Blue Pimpernel

Anagallis arvensis, (ssp coerulea) (AP 77)

Like Scarlet Pimpernel
but with blue flowers
and narrower leaves.
Height - 25 cms

Bog Pimpernel

Anagallis tenella (AP 77)

Very low growing and
mat forming. Flowers in
pink with darker veins.
Leaves in pairs. Grows
in very wet conditions.
Height - 10 cms

Sea Milkwort

Glaux maritima (AP 77)

Not a true Milkwort. Low growing fleshy compact mat of elliptical leaves. Flowers pale
pink; it is the sepals that are showing not the petals. Flowers grow at the base of leaves.
Height - 20 cms

THE PRIMROSE FAMILY Cont'd...

Brookweed

Samolus valerandi (AP 78)

Spike of small (2 mms across) white flowers. Sepals wrap round seed cases and project above it. Basal rosette of leaves. Stem leaves spoon-shaped.

Height - 40 cms

Cyclamen

Cyclamen hederifolium (AP 76)

Flowers pink/purple. Petals turned back, exposing stigma and stamens. Leaves toothed and mottled. After flowering, stem coils to bring seedhead to the ground. *Height - 15 cms*

Eastern Cyclamen

Cyclamen coum (AP 76)

Petals slightly rounder with a dark patch at the base. Leaves kidney shaped.
Height - 15 cms

Cyclamen

Cyclamen repandum (AP 76)

Slightly larger (25 cms). Flowers deep pink purple but without the dark patch. Leaves toothed.
Height - 25 cms

THE KARO FAMILY   PITTOSPORACEAE

There is only one member of this family recorded in the County.

Kohuhu   **Pittosporum tenuifolium** **(AP 78)**

An evergreen shrub with dark green curled-edged leaves.
Flowers five petalled dark-chocolate with yellow stamens. *Height - 3 metres*

THE HYDRANGEA FAMILY   HYDRANGEACEAE

Although the garden hydrangea is widely planted, it is only quoted in the *Atlas* as from one site, a stream bank.

Mock-orange   **Philadelphus coronarius** **(AP 78)**

A deciduous shrub. Flowers of four white, strongly scented flowers. *Height - 3 metres*

THE CURRANT FAMILY   GROSSULARIACEAE

Apart from Escallonia, the members of this family are those bushes that are thought of as "soft fruit".

Escallonia   **Escallonia macrantha** **(AP 78)**

Evergreen shrub with glossy green leaves.
Flowers have five pink petals which join at the base to form a tube. Leaves oval, toothed and with a slightly sticky feel.
Height - 3 metres

Gooseberry   Ribes uva-crispa   (AP 79)

Deciduous spiky shrub.
Leaves glossy green and deeply lobed.
Flowers green and pendant; petals
soon turn back. Fruit edible berry.
Height - 1.5 metres

Black Currant   Ribes nigrum   (AP 79)

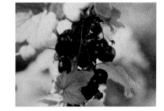

Leaves large (6 cms) and
usually three lobed;
distinctive smell. Yellow/
green flowers hang down
in clusters. Fruit is a
cluster of black berries.
Height - 1.5 metres

Red Currant   Ribes rubrum   (AP 78)

Very similar to Black
Currant but the leaves are
smaller (4 cms). Does not
have distinctive smell.
Fruit is a drooping
cluster of red berries.
Height - 2 metres

Flowering Currant   Ribes sanguineum   (AP 79)

Large clusters of hanging red/pink flowers. Fruit, when set, small purple berries.
Leaves with 3 or 5 lobes. *Height - 2 metres*

THE STONECROP FAMILY   CRASSULACEAE

Usually associated with rocky/stony habitats. Low growing with fleshy leaves which are close together and often in whorls. Flowers usually in compact heads; the individual flowers typically having five petals and ten stamens. Frequently reproduce by runners or prostrate rooting side-branches.

The following three members show outstanding features which distinguish them from the rest of the family. This is emphasised in that their common names does not carry the "stonecrop surname".

Navelwort (Wall Pennywort)   Umbilicus rupestris (AP 80)

Height - 3 metres

Nearly always on walls or rocks. Rounded leaves with the leaf stalk near the centre of the blade. Spires of tubular white/cream/greenish flowers on long stems.

House-leek   Sempervivum tectorum (AP 80)

Height - 40 cms

Tight rosette of fleshy leaves. Leaf tip ends in a spike. Flowering stem emerges from centre of rosette and carries pink star-shaped flowers in a cluster at the top. Whole plant often has a reddish look.

Lamb's-tail   Chiastophyllum oppositifolium (AP 79)

Rosette of fleshy oval toothed leaves. Dark red/brown stem carrying drooping 'tails' of yellow flowers. *Height - 20 cms*

THE STONECROP FAMILY Cont'd...

Apart from Orpine, the remainder of this Family all carry the name 'Stonecrop'. The first seven are all low growing i.e. below 25 cms.

Mossy Stonecrop   **Crassula tillaea   (AP 79)**

A very small (2-3 cms) ground hugging plant. The leaves become bright red. The flowers are extremely small and white or pale pink. Occurs on bare sandy soil, usually on the coast.
Height - 2-3 cms

White Stonecrop   **Sedum album   (AP 81)**

Flowers without pinkish tinge, on distinct stems. Leaves are alternate, fleshy and stubby; sometimes pink after drought. Flower cluster forms a domed head.

Height - 10 cms

English Stonecrop   **Sedum anglicum (AP 81)**

Flowers white with pink tinge on very short stems. Five petals giving plant a 'starry' appearance.

Leaves are alternate, fleshy and stubby.
Height - 5 cms

THE STONECROP FAMILY Cont'd...

Thick-leaved Stonecrop   Sedum dasyphyllum (AP 81)

Leaves opposite. Leaves grey,
downy and more spaced.
Flowers white but pink underside.

The *Atlas* also records three yellow flowered species:-

Biting Stonecrop   Sedum acre (AP 81)

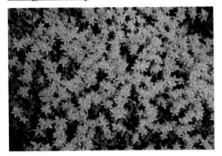 

The smallest of the yellow flowered
species, forming a low mat (6 cms).
Flowers with five petals.

Leaves very small, bright green,
close to the stem.
Height - 6 cms

Reflexed Stonecrop   Sedum rupestre (AP 80)

  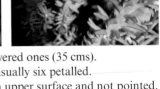

The largest of the yellow flowered ones (35 cms).
Flowers 15 mms across and usually six petalled.
Leaves grey/green, not flat on upper surface and not pointed.
Old leaves are not persistent.
Height - 25 cms

Rock Stonecrop

Sedum forsterianum (AP 81)

Mat forming with grey/green leaves flattened above, and pointed.
Flowers 10 mms across and usually seven petalled. Flower head is slightly domed and old leaves persist on the stem. Non-flowering shoots have leaves in a terminal cluster.
Height - 25 cms

The *Atlas* describes five pink flowered stonecrops; all of them are classed as rare or very rare.

Orpine

Sedum telephium (AP 80)

Tall (60 cms) with rounded head of pink flowers. Often found in woodland shade. Leaves broad, fleshy and toothed; alternate on stem which is often a reddish colour.
Height - 60 cms

Butterfly Stonecrop

Sedum spectabile   (AP 80)

Tall (50 cms) with a large
domed head of pink flowers.
Leaves grey/green, fleshy but either
opposite or in whorls, almost stalkless.
Height - 50 cms

Caucasian Stonecrop

Sedum spurium   (AP 80)

Low growing, mat forming.
Leaves rounded and toothed.
Height - 15 cms

Rounded pink flowers heads.
Individual petals about 1 cm.

THE SAXIFRAGE FAMILY   SAXIFRAGACEAE

Relatively low growing plants, usually with a basal rosette of leaves and a leafless stem. Apart from Golden Saxifrages, they have five petals. Golden Saxifrages have no petals but four sepals.

Elephant-ears   **Bergenia crassifolia   (AP 82)**

Stout prostate thick stem. Large (20 cms) leaves; leaves oval/round shaped. Flowers form a round head on a central stem, head often droops. *Height - 30 cms*

Heart-leaved Bergenia   **Bergenia cordifolia   (AP 82)**

Leaves heart-shaped. Flower head usually upright and often branched. *Height - 40 cms*

Mossy Saxifrage   **Saxifraga hypnoides   (AP 83)**

Mat forming with very fine leaves. White flowers with five petals. *Height - 20 cms*

126

THE SAXIFRAGE FAMILY Cont'd....

Rue-leaved Saxifrage
(Three-fingered Saxifrage)

Saxifraga tridactylites   (AP 83)

Sticky, hairy annual. Flower stalk branches relatively low down.
Distinctive shaped leaves. White, five petalled flowers.
Height - 10 cms

Londonpride

Saxifraga x urbium (AP 82)

Spray of small, pale-pink starry flowers, carried high above the leaves. Stem leafless,
pink and upright. Basal rosette of round leaves. Leaves have numerous small teeth on a
translucent border. *Height - 30 cms*

Lesser Londonpride

Saxifraga cuneifolia (AP 82)

Similar to Londonpride but smaller whiter flowers. Leaves 1 cm across and less toothed.
Pale border to leaf is very narrow. *Height - 20 cms*

THE SAXIFRAGE FAMILY Cont'd....

Meadow Saxifrage   **Saxifraga granulata   (AP 82)**

Largest of the 'saxifrage' plants. Flowers about 2.5 cms across, each have
5 white petals. Leaves deeply lobed. Bulbils around basal rosette.
Height - 50 cms

The four remaining saxifrages all have yellow flowers.

Pick-a-back-plant   **Tolmiea menziesii   (AP 83)**

Has 60 cms spikes of brown/yellow spiky flowers.
Flowers four petalled. Leaves light green, heart-shaped with jagged teeth.
Height - 60 cms

Fringe-cups   **Tellima grandiflora   (AP 83)**

Leaves round
and toothed.
Five jagged
petals
protruding
from cup-
shaped sepals.
Height - 60 cms

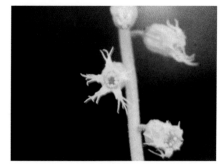

THE SAXIFRAGE FAMILY Cont'd....

Opposite-leaved Golden-saxifrage   **Chrysosplenium oppositifolium** (AP 83)

Low creeping habit. Square stems. Leaves on short stalks form a mat usually at stream edges. Leaves rounded and opposite. Flowers made up of four yellow/green sepals, 4 mms across. *Height - 15 cms*

Alternate-leaved Golden-saxifrage   **Chrysosplenium alternifolium** (AP 83)

Low creeping habit, often at stream edge.
Stems triangular. Leaves toothed, heart-shaped
and alternate. Longer leaf stalks.
Flower made up of four yellow/green sepals, 6 mms across.
Height - 15 cms

THE ROSE FAMILY   ROSACEAE

A very large family which includes trees e.g. Cherry; shrubs e.g. Dog-rose and herbaceous plants such as Silverweed. Excluding hybrids, extreme rarities and by grouping together those plants which are acknowledged to be very difficult to identify, it is possible to reduce the number to be considered. However, this leaves nearly sixty species. For this reason we have divided the family into three groups – trees, shrubs and herbaceous plants.

Group 1 Trees i.e. those which, left to grow naturally, have a distinct trunk.

Rowan   **Sorbus aucuparia** (AP 99)

Smallish tree with pinnate
leaves. White flowers
carried in a compact head.
Clusters of red berries, (one
of the first trees to show
ripe berries). Smooth grey
bark. *Height - 15 metres*

Whitebeam   **Sorbus   (AP 99 & 100)**

We have used this title to cover several closely related species, most of which are rare and very difficult to identify. In general smallish trees with dull white flowers in a domed head. Berries produced later are usually red. The pale green leaves have distinct veins and, depending on the species, are toothed to some extent. *Height - 15 metres*

Hawthorn   **Crataegus monogyna   (AP 102)**

Flat topped spray of white flowers, which fade to pink. Leaves strongly lobed, three or five times. Clusters of small red berries, (haws). Spiney. Young leaves have red stalks. *Height - 10 metres*

Medlar   **Mespilus germanica   (AP 102)**

Long oval leaves. Flowers (with five white petals), usually in ones and twos along the branch like an untidy Dog-rose. Fruit large (3 cms across) and green with 'open end'. Older trees may have spines. *Height - 10 metres*

THE ROSE FAMILY   Group 1   Cont'd...

Apple

Malus domestica (AP 99)

A variable tree depending on variety (in gardening terms). Leaves oval pointed, downy at first. Flowers white/pink (apple blossom) spread along the branches. Fruit large, depending on variety (av. 7 cms). *Height - 15 metres*

Crab Apple

Malus sylvestris (AP 99)

Flowers pale pink in small clusters. Leaves oval, toothed and downy at first. Fruit small, 2-3 cms, yellow/green with reddish flushes.*Height - 10 metres*

Pear

Pyrus communis (AP 98)

White flowers in clusters. Leaves a pointed oval. Fruit typical pear-shaped. Bark often broken into square blocks. *Height - 20 metres*

Bird Cherry   Prunus padus (AP 98)

Creamy white flowers in long tassels, (sometimes drooping). Leaves oval and narrow with hairs on underside by the midrib. Fruit shiny black about 7 mms.
Height - 15 metres

Blackthorn   Prunus spinosa (AP 97)

Very thorny. Flowers emerge late March before the leaves. Flowers white about 12 mms across. Flowers strung out along the branches.

Fruit is the very black sloe. Suckers very freely.
Height - 4 metres

Wild Plum - Bullace   Prunus domestica (AP 97)

Bullace is regarded as a sub-species of the Wild Plum. The plum is the less thorny of the two. Fruit purple/black but larger than the Sloe. White flowers in small clusters. Twigs downy when young.
Height - 8 metres

THE ROSE FAMILY   Group 1   Cont'd...

Cherry Plum   **Prunus cerasifers (AP 97)**

Flowers white and usually solitary, aligned along the branch. Twigs hairless and glossy green. Flowers and leaves emerge at the same time, (as early as February). Normally thornless. Fruit is yellow or red. *Height - 8 metres*

Wild Cherry   **Prunus avium (AP 97)**

Despite the 'avium' in it's name, this is not the Bird Cherry. White flowers in small clusters. Petals slightly notched. Leaf stalk is red above and yellow below. Leaves coppery when young. Fruit reddish. Bark often has horizontal lines. *Height - 25 metres*

Group 2

Bushes, i.e. those which have a number of stems or branches rising from about ground level and where the height rarely exceeds five or six metres.

Kerria   **Kerria japonica (AP 85)**

Flowers, often double, bright yellow. Stems cane-like and suckering freely. Leaves oval, pointed and toothed.

Height - 3 metres

THE ROSE FAMILY Group 2 Cont'd...

Firethorn   Pyracantha coccinea (AP 101)

Sprays of white flowers which produce bright red or orange/yellow berries.
Extremely spiny.

Leaves small (5 cms) oval, narrow and toothed. Leaf stalks hairy.
Height - 3 metres

Cherry Laurel   Prunus laurocerasus (AP 98)

Erect broad
spikes of
white flowers.

Evergreen with large, glossy leathery
leaves, very slightly toothed.
Height - 7 metres

Clusters of
large black
fruits.

THE ROSE FAMILY Group 2 Cont'd...

Brambles Rubus species.

The *Atlas* lists some 80 different species of Rubus or Bramble. It also makes the point that they are very difficult to identify and in many cases are only known from one or two sites. For these reasons, we have limited the descriptions to include only the Raspberry, the Bramble, and the Dewberry.

Raspberry

Rubus idaeus (AP 85)

Usually fresh, upright canes emerge each year; in mild Winters canes remain and put out side branches in Spring. Flowers white/green in loose sprays. Fruit - the red raspberry. Leaves have three leaflets. Stems have weak thorns.
Height - 2 metres

Bramble (Blackberry)

Rubus fruticosus (AP 85-90)

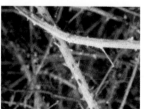

Long stems, which arch, dip down and often root at the tip. Very thorny. Flowers in clusters with white petals. Fruit is the blackberry. Leaves divided into three (sometimes five) strongly, toothed leaflets.
Height - 2 metres

THE ROSE FAMILY Group 2 Cont'd...

Dewberry   **Rubus caesius   (AP 90)**

More prostrate than Bramble and less prickly; forms a low mat. Flowers very similar to Bramble but the fruit has fewer 'segments' (up to five). The fruit ripens to black but it is often covered in a white bloom.
Height - 1 metre

Cotoneasters. There are many species; the *Atlas* refers to fourteen species (or sub-species). Most of these are very rare and limited to one or two shrubs. The four species most likely to be seen are-

Wall Cotoneaster   **Cotoneaster horizontalis   (AP 101)**

Frequently found growing vertically against a wall. Distinct 'herring-bone' pattern to the side branches. Flowers pale pink, 4 mm, 'tulip-shaped'. Berries bright red.
Height - 2 metres

THE ROSE FAMILY Group 2 Cont'd...

Small-leaved Cotoneaster

Cotoneaster integrifolius   (AP 100)

Small leaves clustered tightly along the stem. Flowers white with open petals (10 mms across) and with very dark stamens. Red berries in ones and twos.
Height - 1 metre

Himalayan Cotoneaster

Cotoneaster simonsii   (AP 101)

Tall (4 metres). Flowers pale pink with a red patch. Leaves broad oval and pointed, downy on underside. Berries orange, usually in ones and twos.
Height - 4 metres

Franchet's Cotoneaster

Cotoneaster franchetii   (AP 101)

Loose, pliable twigs. Leaves broad oval and pointed at the tip.
Height - 3 metres

Berries red and in small clusters (up to six).

Japanese Quince
Maule's Quince

Chaenomeles japonica   (AP 98)
Chaenomeles speciosa   (AP 98)

There is a lot of confusion about names. Old gardening books refer to these plants as 'Cydonia' but this term is now restricted to the true Quince which has white or pale pink flowers and a pear shaped yellow fruit. The two Chaenomeles have been known as Japonica or Japanese Quince. They are thorny and have bright red flowers. The fruit is rounded, peach like. *Height - 3 metres*

Bridewort   Spiraea salicifolia   (AP 84)

Deciduous shrub which suckers freely to make thickets. Flowers white or pink in a 'bottle-brush' shaped head. Leaves long, narrow and toothed. Fruit is dry, not a hip or berry. *Height - 2 metres*

Roses   Rosa species   (AP 94)

Another complex group with a number of hybrids and some very rare examples. Of the 25 plants mentioned in the *Atlas*, we have limited this work to the five species most likely to be seen.

Field-rose   Rosa arvensis   (AP 94)

The styles form a column in the centre of the flower. Petals creamy white; flower about 4 cms across. Stamens turn brown. After the petals die, the sepals form a clear star pattern before they too die. The style persists as a 'beak' on top of the hip. *Height - 2 metres*

Burnet Rose   **Rosa pimpinellifolia   (AP 94)**

Low growing (30 cms) and suckering to form patches. Flowers cream-white about 3 cms across. Hips dark purple and with persistent styles. Leaves made up of five to seven rounded leaflets. *Height - 30 cms*

Japanese Rose   **Rosa rugosa   (AP 95)**

Large flowered (6 cms); and usually in shades of pink/reddish purple. Hips large, red and with sepals present. Extremely thorny. *Height - 2 metres*

Dog-rose   **Rosa canina (AP 95)**

Arching stem with backward pointing curved thorns. Flowers pink or white, 45mms across. The dark green leaves have several pairs of toothed leaflets. The seeds are in red hips which soon lose the sepals. *Height - 3 metres*

Sweet-briar (Eglantine)   Rosa rubiginosa (AP 96)

Pink flowers, 30 mms
across. Stalked glands on
leaves and flower stalks.
Hips red with sepals falling
early. *Height - 2 metres*

Group 3

The herbaceous members of the Rose Family can be further divided into two; those that
have "ordinary" flowers with obvious petals etc. and those whose petals are small or
even absent.

Those with obvious flowers

Meadowsweet   Filipendula ulmaria (AP 84)

Height - 1 metre

A tall (1 m) plant with head of many small white flowers. Flowers strongly scented. Leaves
pinnate, leaflets toothed and paired. Central stalk of leaflets red. Pair of very small leaflets
between each large pair. Plant of damp meadows. At a distance, Meadowsweet is not
unlike Meadow-rue, the leaves however are very different. See page 21.

Dropwort   Filipendula vulgaris (AP 84)

Very like Meadowsweet. Leaves much more divided,
'fern-like'. The individual flowers slightly larger.
Plant of dry grassland. *Height - 80 cms*

THE ROSE FAMILY Group 3 Cont'd...

Marsh Cinquefoil

Potentilla palustris (AP 90)

Flowers brown/purple. Narrow pointed
petals which open to star-shape.
Leaves palmate. Grows in water or
on very wet ground.
Height - 50 cms

Water Avens

Geum rivale (AP 92)

Flowers pink/purple/brown, bell-shaped and pendant. Leaves rounded and lobed or
divided into three leaflets. Seeds in a bur-like head. Grows in water or in very wet
ground. *Height - 50 cms*

Barren Strawberry

Potentilla sterilis (AP 91)

The flowers are white with five petals. The petals are slightly notched and there are
noticeable gaps between the petals. It does not produce edible berries.
Height - 15 cms

Wild Strawberry   Fragaria vesca (AP 91)

Flowers with five white
petals but no gaps
between the petals.
Petals un-notched.
Fruit a small strawberry.
Height - 20 cms

The following all have yellow flowers

Agrimony   Agrimonia eupatoria (AP 92)

Almost leafless spikes of closely-packed five petalled yellow flowers. Lower leaves
pinnate and softly hairy. Slightly scented. Seed cases are small burs.
Height - 80 cms

Fragrant Agrimony   Agrimonia procera (AP 92)

Similar to Agrimony but larger (1 metre). More fragrant. Pinnate stem leaves are larger
and more numerous than on Agrimony. They are deeply toothed. Seed cases have
hooked burs. Flowers less densely packed along the spike.
Height - 1m

Yellow-flowered Strawberry

Flowers solitary and yellow. Leaves made up of three leaflets.

Duchesnea indica (AP 92)

Fruit a red strawberry.

Silverweed

Prostrate with pinnate leaves. Leaves silvery especially on underside.
Height - 15 cms

Potentilla anserina (AP 90)

Flowers yellow, solitary and long stalked. Flowers 20 mms across.

Hoary Cinquefoil

More upright and fleshy than the other cinquefoils. Leaves pinnate and toothed.
Height - 70 cms

Potentilla argentea (AP 90)

Yellow flowers with petals longer than sepals.

Tormentil

Yellow flower with four notched petals.
Creeping stems which do not root.
Height - 30 cms

Potentilla erecta   (AP 90)

Leaves palmate and with stipules
at the base.

Trailing Tormentil

Creeping stem which does root.
Flowers yellow with four or five petals.
Height - 40 cms

Potentilla anglica   (AP 91)

Small stipules and distinct leaf stalk.

Sulphur Cinquefoil

More upright and fleshy than the other
cinquefoils. *Height - 70 cms*

Potentilla recta   (AP 90)

Leaves pinnate and toothed.
Yellow flowers with petals longer
than sepals.

Spring Cinquefoil

Yellow flowers in small clusters. Low creeping stem. *Height - 10 cms*

Creeping Cinquefoil

Creeping runners which root and are usually reddish. Leaves hairless. They are palmate and toothed.

Wood Avens

Flowers yellow, petals longer than sepals but spaced so that sepals are visible.
Height - 70 cms

Potentilla neumanniana (AP 90)

Upper leaves unstalked, all leaves much divided.

Potentilla reptans (AP 91)

Flowers yellow, solitary and with small toothed sepals. Long lower stalk.
Height - 20 cms but runners can be much longer.

Geum urbanum (AP 92)

Leaves with three or four leaflets.
Seed case has hooked burs.

145

Plants without 'conventional' flowers

Great Burnet

Sanguisorba officinalis   (AP 93)

Flowers tiny but the mass of them form a red/purple oval flower-head.

Leaves pinnate with long- stalked leaflets. *Height - 1 metre*

Salad Burnet

Sanguisorba minor (AP 93)

Flower heads small (15 mms) and round. *Height - 40 cms*

Leaves pinnate with many pairs of leaflets. Has basal rosette of leaves.

Fodder Burnet, (a sub species) occasionally can be found. It is like Salad Burnet but the leaves are more deeply toothed.

Pale Lady's-mantle

Alchemilla xanthochlora (AP 93)

Three species with the same common name.

Small flowers, green/yellow in clusters. Colour comes from yellow stamens. Stem and leaf stalk densely hairy but leaves hairless above. Leaves with rounded lobes; lobes with sharply pointed equal teeth. *Height - 50 cms*

THE ROSE FAMILY Group 3 Cont'd...

Southern Lady's-mantle   **Alchemilla filicaulis (AP 93)**

Now rare, and mostly in west of County. Whole plant downy.
Leaves with 7 to 9 rounded toothed lobes but sides of lobes often folded downwards.
Base of leaf stalk reddish.

Garden Lady's-mantle   **Alchemilla mollis (AP 94)**

The garden form. Leaves large (14 cms) with teeth pointed and incurved.
Height - 10 cms

Parsley-piert   **Aphanes arvensis (AP 94)**

Flowers very small (1 mm), without petals. Leaves grey/green almost stalkless. Leaves
have fan-shaped stipules very close to leaf blade. Stipules have triangular lobes. Pods,
each one dumb-bell shaped, arranged on the stem like a miniature bunch of grapes.
Height - 10 cms

Slender Parsley-piert   **Aphanes inexspectata (AP 94)**

Very similar to the common species but slightly more delicate. The seed pod does not
have a waist.

147

THE PEA FAMILY   FABACEAE

The flowers of this family have five petals arranged so that the top petal stands up and becomes the standard, two side petals become the wings and the two lowest petals become the keel.

Unfortunately it is another large group and, allowing for the usual exceptions, the *Atlas* recognises over 60 species.

To identify the plants as well as the flower itself, an examination of leaves, tendrils, pods and the shape of the flower head all play a part.

Flower colour can also present a problem in that different people put a different interpretation on the colours in the pale-pink, purple, lilac shades. It is also a problem in that different petals on the same flower can be in different shades and these shades can alter as the flower ages.

Group 1   Trees

Laburnum   **Laburnum anagyroides (AP 113)**

Flowers in yellow hanging trusses. A small deciduous tree. Leaves trefoil, leaflets oval and pointed. Seeds in long, downwards hanging pods.
Height - 10 metres

THE PEA FAMILY Group 1 Cont'd....

False-acacia   **Robinia pseudoacacia (AP 103)**

A deciduous tree to 20 metres. Leaves pinnate, leaflets oval. White flowers in pendant trusses. Twigs especially are spiny. *Height - 20 metres*

Group 2 Shrubs

Gorse   **Ulex europaeus (AP 114)**

Spiny shrub; 2 metres in height. Spines strongly grooved.
Yellow flowers in Spring. Hairy sepals just over half the length of the petals.
Height - 2 metres

Western Gorse   **Ulex gallii (AP 114)**

Spiny shrub; 1.5 metres in height. Spines lightly grooved.
Yellow flowers in Summer and Autumn. Sepals less hairy, nearly as long as petals.
Height - 1.5 metres

Petty Whin   Genista anglica (AP 113)

Low shrub; 1 metre in height.
Yellow flowers with the keel longer
than the standard. Flowers in small
clusters at the end of the branches,
strong spines.
Height - 1 metre

Dyer's Greenweed   Genista tinctoria (AP 113)

Small non-spiny shrub; height to 80 cms.   Yellow flowers in loose spike. Keel and
Leaves long and narrow.   standards are same length.
Height - 80 cms

Broom   Cytisus scoparius (AP 113)

Deciduous spineless shrub; height to 2 metres. Small trefoil leaves which quickly fall
leaving green stems. Stem ridged. Flower petals yellow and held more open than other
similar shrubs. *Height - 2 metres*

THE PEA FAMILY Cont'd….

Group 3   Low herbaceous plants with tendrils, tendrils usually branched.

Broad-leaved Everlasting-pea

Lathyrus latifolius (AP 107)

Much the tallest of this group (3 metres).
Leaves in single pairs.
Stems winged. *Height - 3 metres*

Flowers 6 to 8 on long stalk; flowers
red/pink. Branched tendrils.

Narrow-leaved Everlasting pea

Lathyrus sylvestris (AP 107)

Up to two metres in height. Paired leaves
smaller than Broad-leaved.

Flowers pale green/pink. Branched
tendrils. *Height - 2 metres*

Tufted Vetch

Vicia cracca (AP 105)

Pinnate leaves
with many
leaflets. Ending
in branched
tendrils.
Blue/purple
flowers in one
sided spike.
Height - 2 metres

THE PEA FAMILY   Group 3 Cont'd....

Yellow Vetchling   Lathyrus aphaca   (AP 108)

Broad, inverted-shield-shaped stipules in pairs and looking like leaves. True leaves are modified to be tendrils. Yellow flowers borne singly. *Height - 40 cms*

Meadow Vetchling   Lathyrus pratensis (AP 107)

Yellow flowers. Flower head has up to ten flowers. One pair of narrow leaflets. May or may not have tendrils. *Height - 1 metre*

Wood Vetch   Vicia sylvatica   (AP 105)

Flower truss with white flowers with purple markings. Leaves pinnate with many leaflets and branched tendrils. The stipules at the base of the leaf stalk are distinctively spikey. *Height - 2 metres*

THE PEA FAMILY   Group 3 Cont'd….

Bush Vetch

Vicia sepium (AP 106)

About six pairs of small leaflets.
Flowers dull blue/lilac.
Height - 60 cms

Flowers in small clusters.
Branched tendrils.

Common Vetch

Vicia sativa   (AP 106)

Bright red/purple flowers in ones or twos.
Height - 70 cms

About six pairs of leaflets, each leaflet
with a small notch at the top. Branched
tendrils.

Marsh Pea

Lathyrus palustris (AP 107)

Large, 2 cms, blue/purple flowers.
2 to 3 flowers per head.
Height - 1.5 metres

2 to 3 pairs of leaflets.
Limited to wet meadows.

Bithynian Vetch   Vicia bithynica (AP 106)

Flowers blue with whitish keel.
1 or 2 flowers per head.
Leaves divided into 2 or 3
leaflets. Has a very spiky and
obvious stipule at the base
of the leaf stalk.
Height - 60 cms

Spring Vetch   Vicia lathyroides (AP 106)

Small (20 cms). 2 to 4 pairs of leaflets.
Flowers small (6 mms) red/purple
and solitary or in pairs.
Tendrils usually un-branched.
Found on coastal sandy areas.
Height - 20 cms

Fyfield (Tuberous) Pea   Lathyrus tuberosus   (AP 107)

Tendril
usually
branched
near tip of
leaf. Leaf
made up of
one pair of
leaflets.

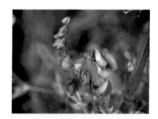

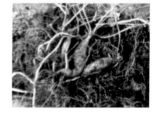

Tall (2 metres) and straggly. Flowers   Has root
red/purple, about four per head in loose   tubers.
spikes. *Height - climbing to 2 metres*

THE PEA FAMILY   Group 3 Cont'd....

Tares

Tares have small flowers on long stalks and have narrow leaflets.

Hairy Tare   Vicia hirsuta (AP 105)

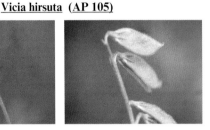

Tends to form a loose clump. Small, dull lilac/blue flowers in clusters averaging about
five or six. Leaves made up of about six narrow leaflets. Pods downy.
Height - 10 cms

Smooth Tare   Vicia tetrasperma (AP 106)

Flowers pale purple/pink, 1 or 2 per head.
Leaves usually with 2 to 4 pairs of long
leaflets. Tendrils are usually unbranched.
Height - 80 cms

Slender Tare   Vicia parviflora (AP 105)

Flowers usually blue/pink with up to 4 per flower head.
Leaves made up of a few pairs of long narrow leaflets. Tendrils usually branched.
Height - 60 cms

THE PEA FAMILY   Cont'd....

Group 4

Plants in this group have pinnate leaves ending in a leaflet and not a tendril.

<u>**Wild Liquorice**</u>   <u>**Astragalus glycyphyllos**</u> **(AP 103)**

Flowers greenish cream. Many flowers forming a spike. About 5 pairs of broad oval leaflets. Stems often zigzag. The seed pods form a distinctive cluster. *Height - 1 metre*

<u>**Broad Bean**</u>   <u>**Vicia faba**</u> **(AP 107)**

Usually a garden escape. Flowers white in small clusters along the stem. Leaflets large and broad. Pod contains the edible beans. *Height - 1.5 metres*

<u>**Bird's-foot**</u>   <u>**Ornithopus perpusillus**</u> **(AP 104)**

Many leaflets. Sprawling plant. Leaves with numerous small leaflets. Small pink flowers with a yellow lower petal. Pods clearly beaked. *Height - 30 cms*

THE PEA FAMILY   Group 4 Cont'd....

Crown Vetch

Securigera varia   (AP 104)

Flowers pink and white; many in compact radiating heads. The pinnate leaf usually has about 6 pairs of leaflets. The pods are noticeably beaded.
Height - 1 metre

Kidney Vetch

Anthyllis vulneraria   (AP 103)

Flower heads in pairs, yellow with downy, fluffy appearance. Brown sepals.
Many flowers in a flat head. Very occasionally pink/red forms occur.
About four pairs of leaflets with large terminal leaflet.
Height - 60 cms

Horseshoe Vetch

Hippocrepis comosa   (AP 104)

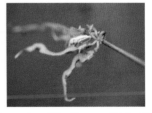

Flowers yellow with about eight or nine in a head. About five pairs of leaflets each toothed and slightly notched. Pods radiating outwards and curly.
Height - 40 cms

THE PEA FAMILY Cont'd….

Group 5 Plants in this group have pairs of leaflets but neither terminal leaflets not tendrils.

Bitter-vetch   **Lathyrus linifolius   (AP 107)**

Flowers red/green with 2 to 4 in a spike.
Stem winged.
Leaflets end in a small point.
Height - 40 cms

Group 6 Leaflets in threes; clovers etc.

The plants in this group have one pair of leaflets/stipules at the base of each leaf stalk and three leaflets (trefoil).

Bird's-foot-trefoil   **Lotus corniculatus   (AP 104)**

Flowers yellow with touches of red; hence alternative name of bacon and eggs. Flowers five to six in a head. Leaves divided into five leaflets. Compact growth form. Pods radiate outwards from top of stem. *Height - 40 cms*

Greater Bird's-foot-trefoil   **Lotus pedunculatus   (AP 104)**

Very similar flower to the common form but plant has straggly climbing growth form and flowers are less bunched. Flowers yellow without red markings. Leaves divided into five pointed leaflets. *Height - 1 metre*

158

THE PEA FAMILY   Group 6 Cont'd….

Lucerne   Medicago sativa (AP 109)

Tall and bushy (90 cms) with
blue/purple flowers.
Flowers in a terminal spike
rather than radiating
outwards like a crown.
Height - 90 cms

The Medicks

These all have yellow flowers, seed pods in clusters and a sprawling habit.

Spotted Medick   Medicago arabica (AP 110)

Sprawling with small groups of yellow
flowers. Leaves have black marks around
their mid-vein.

Large spiky stipules. Pods are coiled.
Height - 50 cms

Toothed Medick   Medicago polymorpha (AP 110)

Similar to Spotted Medick but with smaller, spotless leaves. Stipules spiky.
Pods spiky and coiled. *Height - 50 cms*

THE PEA FAMILY   Group 6 Cont'd….

Black Medick   **Medicago lupulina   (AP 109)**

Cluster of many yellow flowers forming a compact head. Seed pods coiled and black.
Young growth especially downy. *Height - 50 cms*

Melilots

These have yellow or white flowers but are tall and much more upright.

White Melilot   **Melilotus albus   (AP 109)**

Tall (1.5 metres). Flowers white on long spikes. Leaflets long, toothed oval.
Height - 1.5 metres

Tall Melilot   **Melilotus altissimus   (AP 109)**

Tall (1.5 metres). Flowers
yellow on long spike.
All the petals about equal
in length. Pods green,
later becoming black.
Leaflets long narrow oval
and toothed.
Height - 1.5 metres

Ribbed Melilot

Melilotus officinalis (AP 109)

Very like Tall Melilot but flowers a more lemony colour. Keel petal is shorter than the other petals. Leaves roundish oval and slightly toothed. Pods brown. *Height - 1.5 metres*

Restharrows

Downy, ground hugging plants which forms a dense mat, which was said to be so tough that it "arrested" (i.e. stopped) the harrow.

Common Restharrow

Ononis repens (AP 108)

Pink flowers borne in ones and twos along the stem. Stem tough and rooting along its length. Without spines. Leaflets toothed and hairy. *Height - mat is rarely more than 20 cms but creeping stems can be much longer.*

Spiny Restharrow

Ononis spinosa (AP 108)

More upright than the common form. Pink flowers.
Stem is very spiky and has two lines of hairs. *Height - 70 cms*

Group 7   Trefoils and Clovers

Hop Trefoil   **Trifolium campestre   (AP 111)**

Yellow flowers in heads about 6 mms   Individual flowers and fruits have an
across. Leaflets slightly heart-shaped.   'inflated' appearance.
Height - 30 cms

Lesser Trefoil   **Trifolium dubium   (AP 111)**

Sprawling plant with yellow flower heads   Central leaflets have very small notch at
about 3 mms across.   the top. Pods have a short beak.
Height - 20 cms

Slender Trefoil   **Trifolium micranthum   (AP 111)**

Low sprawling growth. Flower heads consist of three to four flowers in a loose spike.
Leaves very small.
Height - 15 cms

THE PEA FAMILY   Group 7   Cont'd....

Red Clover   Trifolium pratense   (AP 111)

Flowers deep pink in a compact egg shaped head about 3 cms
across. Leaflets not notched, but finely toothed. They usually
have a pale crescent or v shaped mark in the centre.
Height - 60 cms

Zigzag Clover   Trifolium medium   (AP 111)

Flowers a deeper purple/pink than Red
Clover. Leaflets clearly toothed and
narrower, without pale markings.

Stem usually zigzag.
Height - 60 cms

Hare's-foot Clover   Trifolium arvense   (AP 112)

Pink head. The sepal spines make
it look fluffy.

Leaflets narrow and toothed.
Height - 25 cms

163

Strawberry Clover

Pink flowers with inflated sepals which give a false impression of succulence. Flowers persist but soon turn brown.

Trifolium fragiferum   (AP 111)

Leaflets oval and toothed.
Height - 30 cms

Reversed Clover

Pink flowers which have the keel petal at the top and the standard below. Individual flowers tend to curl downwards.

Trifolium resupinatum   (AP 111)

Inflated sepals like Strawberry Clover.
Height - 30 cms

Sea Clover

Small pink flower head surrounded by star-like pattern of sepals. *Height - 30 cms*

Trifolium squamosum   (AP 112)

Flowers heads on short stalks and only about 1 cm across. Leaflets very narrow.

THE PEA FAMILY   Group 7 Cont'd....

Knotted Clover

Trifolium striatum   (AP 112)

Low, sprawling growth with pink flower heads on very short stems.
Flowers about 5 mms across.
Leaflets downy on both sides.
Height - 20 cms

Clustered Clover

Trifolium glomeratum   (AP 110)

Sprawling plant with small rather more open pale pink flower heads.
Flower heads without stalks.
Leaflets slightly fan-shaped.
Height - 20 cms

Alsike Clover

Trifolium hybridum   (AP 110)

More erect than white Clover and flowers tend to be pink and white.
Height - 40 cms

Leaflets do not have whitish patches.
Stems do not root along their length.

Fenugreek (Bird's-foot Clover)

Trifolium ornithopodioides   (AP 110)

A distinctive white flowered Clover. Ground hugging. Leaflets almost triangular, and toothed along the top edge. Flower single or in pairs on short stalks. Standards folded along their length; flowers seem pointed. *Height - 15 cms*

White Clover

Trifolium repens   (AP 110)

Leaflets have pale marks. White flowers, with some brown, on long stalks. Stems prostrate and root along their length. *Height - 40 cms*

Rough Clover

Trifolium scabrum   (AP 112)

Small (6 mms) white flowers. Leaflets have pale markings. Very short stalks so that the flowers seem to sit on the leaves. Sepals give flower a "spiky" look. *Height - 15 cms*

THE PEA FAMILY   Group 7 Cont'd....

Suffocated Clover
Trifolium suffocatum (AP 111)

Very rare, limited to a few sandy areas. Small clumps of toothed leaves grow upwards.
Flowers white and unstalked. Petals often hidden by pointed sepals.
Height - 5 cms

Subterranean Clover
Trifolium subterraneum (AP 113)

Plant low growing with oval leaflets.
Flowers sometimes creamy-white, long
and slender but often sterile and without
petals.

On maturity, stalk turns downwards and
pushes pods into the soil.
Height - 40 cms

Group 8

**Flowers not in clustered heads but either in spires and with pinnate leaves or in ones or twos
and with grass-like leaves.**

Goat's-rue
Galega officinalis (AP 103)

Very different
to the Clovers.
Tall (2 metres).
Leaves pinnate
with a number
of narrow
leaflets.
Flowers white
or with lilac
shades on
long spikes.

Height - 2 metres

THE PEA FAMILY   Group 7 Cont'd....

Sainfoin

Medium height (70 cms).
Pink flowers in a conical spike.

Onobrychis viciifolia (AP 103)

Leaves pinnate with many long narrow
leaflets. *Height - 70 cms*

Grass Vetchling

Lathyrus nissolia (AP 108)

Leaves reduced to little more than mid-ribs, looking grass-like.
Flowers red/purple in ones and twos. On long stalks. Neither leaflets nor tendrils.
Height - 80 cms

THE SEA BUCKTHORN FAMILY   ELAEAGNACEAE

Only one member of this family is included in the *Atlas*.

Sea Buckthorn

Very thorny shrub, up to 3 metres high.
Berries bright orange/red. Deciduous
leaves long and thin and greyish.

Hippophae rhamnoides (AP 114)

Twigs with silvery scales. Flowers very
small and hugging the twigs.
Height - 3 metres

THE WATER-MILFOIL FAMILY   HALORAGACEAE

Submerged, or floating aquatic plants. The much divided leaves have a central 'stem' and numerous side branches. The flowers are carried on aerial spikes.

Parrot's-feather   Myriophyllum aquaticum   (AP 114)

Bright green leaves; some leaves are submerged others are at the water surface or just above it. Leaves much divided and in whorls. An invasive 'throw-out' from aquaria.

Spiked Water-milfoil   Myriophyllum spicatum   (AP 115)

Leaves in whorls of four. Leaves finely divided. Prefers limy or brackish water. Flowers on emergent upright spike. *Length of stem - 2 metres*

The *Atlas* refers to two other Milfoils, both rare.

Alternate Water-milfoil   Myriophyllum alterniflorum   (AP 115)

Smallest of the Water-milfoils with leaves in whorls of three or four. Mainly occurs in the acidic waters on Exmoor. *Length of submerged stem - 1 metre.*

Whorled Water-milfoil   Myriophyllum verticillatum   (AP 114)

This is classed as very rare and in only a few scattered sites. Leaves mostly in whorls of five. *Length of submerged stem - 3 metres.*

THE LOOSESTRIFE FAMILY   LYTHRACEAE

A confusingly named family. Of the two recorded members, Purple Loosestrife is not related to the Yellow Loosestrife and Water Purslane is not related to the other Purslanes.

Purple Loose-strife   Lythrum salicaria (AP 115)

Height - 1.5 metres

Tall (1.5 metres) showy plant of late Summer. Flowers are spikes of six-petalled bright purple flowers. Leaves long, narrow and not toothed. Usually near water.

Water Purslane   Lythrum portula (AP 115)

Creeping with stem rooting at intervals. Fleshy spoon-shaped leaves. Flowers small (1mm) and pink, but sometimes without petals. Flowers at the base of the leaves. Usually near water. *Height - 25 cms*

THE DAPHNE FAMILY   THYMELAEACEAE

Only one member of this family is recorded as now present.

Spurge-laurel   Daphne laureola (AP 116)

Small (1 metre) evergreen shrub. Dark-green, shiny leaves. Flowers yellow/green trumpet shaped in small clusters. *Height - 1.5 metres*

THE WILLOWHERB FAMILY   ONAGRACEAE

Flowers of Willowherb are mainly pink. The seeds are in long thin pods which split
lengthways. The seeds released are carried by the wind and have fluffy 'parachutes'.
Apart from the three species below, the rest of the Family are all very similar
with few obvious differences. Flowers of Evening-primrose are yellow.

Rosebay Willowherb   **Chamerion angustifolium (AP 118)**

Tall (1.5 metres)
and usually
growing in a
clump. Four
unequal red
petals.
Sepals red.

Height - 1.5 metres

Great Willowherb   **Epilobium hirsutum (AP 116)**

Tall, nearly 2 metres, and with large (2.5 cms across) pink
and cream flowers. Has a number of flowers in a loose head.
Stem very downy. Leaves stalkless and a narrow toothed oval
shape. *Height - 2 metres*

THE WILLOWHERB FAMILY Cont'd….

New Zealand Willowherb   Epilobium brunnescens (AP 118)

Creeping, mat forming. Roots at intervals along the prostrate stem. Grows near water.
Leaves round and in opposite pairs. Flowers solitary on vertical stems, flowers pink
about 4 mms across. *Height - 10 cms*

The remaining members of this Family are all very similar with only minor
distinguishing features.

Hoary Willowherb   Epilobium parviflorum (AP 116)

Flowers about 12 mms across, pale pink and petals deeply notched. Spear-shaped leaves.
Downy flower head with few flowers. *Height - 75 cms*

Broad-leaved Willowherb   Epilobium montanum (AP 116)

Leaves broad oval, pointed
and toothed; leaves opposite.
Flowers about 10 mms across.
Stem round and hairless.
Height - 80 cms

THE WILLOWHERB FAMILY Cont'd....

Spear-leaved Willowherb

Epilobium lanceolatum (AP 117)

Leaves alternate
and narrow.
Few flowers;
start white and
turn pink as
they age.

Height - 80 cms

Marsh Willowherb

Epilobium palustre (AP 117)

Height - 60 cms

No stem ridges.
Leaves long and
narrow, tapering
at each end.
Flowers about
6 mms across;
pale pink/white.
Height - 60 cms

Square-stalked Willowherb

Epilobium tetragonum (AP 117)

Stem has four pronounced ridges. Finely toothed, long and
narrow leaves. Pink flowers about 7 mms across.
Pods about 8 cms long.
Height - 1 metre

THE WILLOWHERB FAMILY Cont'd....

Short-fruited Willowherb   **Epilobium obscurum   (AP 117)**

Similar to Square-stalked Willowherb. Leaves broader and yellowish-green. Pods about 5 cms long. *Height– 80 cms*

Pale Willowherb   **Epilobium roseum   (AP 117)**

Similar to Square-stalked Willowherb but stems slightly more round. Petals white streaked with pink. Long leaf stalks. *Height - 80 cms*

American Willowherb   **Epilobium ciliatum (AP 117)**

Stems with raised ridges. Leaves long (10 cms), short stalked and hairless. Flowers about 10 mms across and with spaces between petals. *Height - 1 metre*

Evening Primroses

Are part of the same family as the Willowherbs. They have yellow flowers.

Large-flowered Evening-primrose   **Oenothera glazioviana   (AP 118)**

Flowers are about 7 cms across.
Sepals have red stripes and styles project
beyond the stamen. Stem has red dots
and the leaves are alternate.
Height - 1.8 metres

THE WILLOWHERB FAMILY Cont'd....

Common Evening-primrose

Downy stems without red spots.
Sepals green. *Height - 1.5 metres*

Small-flowered Evening-primrose

Flowers are relatively small (about 2.5 cms across). The sepals are green but the leaf mid-rib is often reddish.

Fragrant Evening-primrose

Flowers are almost 4 cms across and are strongly scented. The style and stamens are almost the same length.

Oenothera biennis (AP 118)

Flowers about 5 cms across.

Oenothera cambrica (AP 119)

Red spots on upper part of stem.
Height - 2 metres

Oenothera stricta (AP 119)

The sepals have a red stripe but the stem has few, if any, red spots.
Height - 80 cms

THE WILLOWHERB FAMILY Cont'd….

Fuchsia

Flowers have red/purple petals and deep red sepals. The stamens and the even longer style protrude beyond the petals. Leaves are toothed, oval and in opposite pairs.

Fuchsia magellanica (AP 119)

Height - 2 metres

Enchanter's-nightshade

Circaea lutetiana (AP 119)

Has small pale pink flowers on a spike. The petals are notched.
The seed cases are down-turned burs. The leaves are oval and in opposite pairs.
Height - 60 cms

THE DOGWOOD FAMILY   CORNACEAE

Shrubs with simple opposite leaves. Flowers have parts in fours and are in an umbel.

Dogwood

Cornus sanguinea (AP 119)

A deciduous shrub with red winter twigs. Leaves are oval with prominent veins.
Flowers are in umbels (clusters) each umbel about 5 cms across. The individual small flowers are white, each with four petals. The fruit is a cluster of berries which turn black.
Height - 4 metres

THE DOGWOOD FAMILY Cont'd....

Cornelian-cherry   Cornus mas (AP 120)

A deciduous shrub with flowers appearing very early in the year before the leaves.
The yellow flowers, about 3 mms across are borne very close to the twig.
Fruit are oval red berries. *Height - 4 metres*

Spotted Laurel   Aucuba japonica (AP 120)

An evergreen shrub with large, glossy, green and yellow leaves. Plants are either
male or female. Female flowers have red berries. *Height - 3 metres*

THE MISTLETOE FAMILY   VISCACEAE

The *Atlas* records only the one member of this family.

Mistletoe   Viscum album (AP 120)

An evergreen semi-parasite found on a variety of trees. It has paired oval leaves and
small green four petalled flowers. Stems remain green. Fruit is a cluster of white sticky
berries. *Height - clump 70 cms across*

THE SPINDLE FAMILY   CELASTRACEAE

Another very small family of shrubs.

Spindle   Euonymus europaeus (AP 120)

A deciduous shrub with four sided twigs. The leaves are oval and toothed.
The flowers are in small clusters, each flower having four small whitish petals.
Fruits are bright pink/red berries. *Height - 3 metres*

Evergreen Spindle   Euonymus japonicus (AP 121)

An evergreen member
of the Spindle group.
Leaves bluntly oval,
often variegated.
Flowers and red berries
like spindle.
Height - 4 metres

THE HOLLY FAMILY   AQUIFOLIACEAE

The *Atlas* only records one species:-.

Holly   Ilex aquifolium (AP 121)

An evergreen with very prickly leaves; leaves dark green and glossy (some cultivated
forms have cream markings on the leaves). Flowers are white petalled and in tight
clusters. Female trees have the traditional red berries.
Height - 20 metres

THE BOX FAMILY

Another "one member" family.

Box

Buxus sempervirens (AP 121)

Evergreen shrub with small, round leaves. Flowers in small clusters with male flower at tip and female flowers below it. Male flower has four sepals, female flower has four sepal-like bracts. Seeds are in a green oval-shaped capsule.
Height - 5 metres

THE SPURGE FAMILY

EUPHORBIACEAE

A family of herbaceous plants all (except Caper Spurge) with alternate simple leaves. Flowers are without petals and either male or female. Flowers of the Mercury species are in spikes, those of the Spurges are in umbels.

Dog's Mercury

Mercurialis perennis (AP 121)

A woodland/ hedgerow plant. The stem creeps (and becomes invasive) below ground, above ground it is unbranched. The flowers are carried on a green spike.
Height - 30 cms

THE SPURGE FAMILY

Annual Mercury

EUPHORBIACEAE

Mercurialis annua (AP 121)

Leaves shiny green and slightly toothed. Stem with side branches giving a bushy appearance. Green flowers in spike. Flower spikes prominent. *Height - 30 cms*

Caper Spurge

Euphorbia lathyris (AP 122)

Grey-green sharp pointed leaves. Leaves opposite in pairs, without stalks and with smooth edges. *Height - 1.5 metres*

Dwarf Spurge

Euphorbia exigua (AP 122)

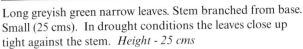

Long greyish green narrow leaves. Stem branched from base. Small (25 cms). In drought conditions the leaves close up tight against the stem. *Height - 25 cms*

Mediterranean Spurge

Euphorbia characias (AP 123)

A grey green plant with strap-shaped leaves. The top of stem bends over in its early growth and straightens as the flowers develop. Yellow/green flowers with stem turning red. *Height - 1 metre*

Varieties of hybrids often appear, self-sown, in gardens. Some varieties are encouraged because of the dark markings on the flowers.

Cypress Spurge

Euphorbia cyparissias (AP 123)

Patch forming with numerous erect stems. Leaves numerous and needle like. Flower heads bright yellow. *Height - 30 cms*

THE SPURGE FAMILY Cont'd...

Sea Spurge

Euphorbia paralias (AP 123)

Usually found on dunes. Clump forming with a number of erect stems. Leaves strap-shaped, thick and grey green. Flowers carried towards the top of the stem. *Height - 60 cms*

Wood Spurge

Euphorbia amygdaloides (AP 123)

Woodland species. Over-wintering rosettes give rise to flowering stems. Leaves dark green and a narrow oval. *Height - 80 cms*

Petty Spurge

Euphorbia peplus (AP 123)

Usually two or three branches. Leaves untoothed. Green flower-heads in flattened clusters. A common garden weed. *Height - 30 cms*

THE SPURGE FAMILY Cont'd...

Sun Spurge   Euphorbia helioscopia (AP 122)

Usually one main stem.
Spoon-shaped leaves,
toothed at the tip; bright
green. Flowers yellow/
green in flattened heads.
A common garden weed.
Height - 40 cms

Broad-leaved Spurge   Euphorbia platyphyllos (AP 122)

Leaves oval with pointed
tip, heart-shaped at base,
toothed. Flower-head
loose giving a bushy
appearance.
Usually branched.
Plant sometimes downy.
The seed pods are
covered in small
swellings.
Height - 70 cms

Upright Spurge   Euphorbia serrulata (AP 122)

An introduced Spurge which occurs at only a very few sites.
The leaves are oval, noticeably pointed and with toothed edges.
Height - 70 cms

THE BUCKTHORN FAMILY   RHAMNACEAE

There are two deciduous shrubs recorded for this Family.

Buckthorn   Rhamnus cathartica (AP 123)

The leaves are oval, toothed and opposite, each with two to four pairs of veins.
The shrubs are thorny. The flowers in small clusters have four greenish petals.
The fruit is a black berry. *Height - 5 metres*

Alder Buckthorn   Frangula alnus (AP 124)

Leaves alternate and untoothed. Leaves with about seven pairs of veins. No thorns.
Flowers with five greenish petals in small clusters. Fruit a berry which is red for a long
time, finally turning black. *Height - 4 metres*

THE VINE FAMILY   VITACEAE

There are two climbers recorded in this Family, the first, Virginia Creeper is especially
rampant.

Virginia-creeper   Parthenocissus quinquefolia (AP 124)

 Leaves so deeply divided
that they appear as 3,5 or 7
leaflets. Climbs with
tendrils ending in 'suckers'.
Fruit is small (1 cm),
blue/black berries.
Striking Autumn colours.
Height - 20 metres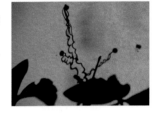

184

THE VINE FAMILY Cont'd...

Grape-vine   **Vitis vinifera   (AP 124)**

Leaves deeply lobed and untoothed. Climbs with tendrils. Fruit is the grape.
Height - 10 metres

THE FLAX FAMILY   ## LINACEAE

Erect, hairless herbaceous plants. Flowers with 4 or 5 parts, white or blue. Fruit is a dry capsule.

Fairy Flax   **Linum catharticum   (AP 124)**

Flowers white in forked clusters. Flowers about 4 mms across. Leaves narrow and in pairs. Each leaf has a single central vein. *Height - 15 cms*

Flax   **Linum usitatissimum   (AP 124)**

Leaves narrow and pointed. Flowers in loose cluster. Flowers 20 mms across.
Petals blue with dark veins. *Height - 60 cms*

THE FLAX FAMILY Cont'd...

Pale Flax   Linum bienne   (AP 124)

Slender stem.
Leaves narrow,
pointed and
three veined.
Flowers pale
blue, about 15
mms across.
Sepals oval.

Height - 50 cms

THE MILKWORT FAMILY   POLYGALACEAE

Low, shrubby plants with distinctive shaped flowers. Flowers in a spike.

Common Milkwort   Polygala vulgaris   (AP 125)

Flower of two large wings and three petals joined to form a small inner tube.
Three small outer sepals. Flowers usually blue but can be pink or white.
Leaves alternate along the stem. *Height - 25 cms*

Heath Milkwort   Polygala serpyllifolia   (AP 125)

Leaves very narrow.
Flowers pale blue and about 6 to 8 along
the flower spike.
Height - 25 cms

THE HORSE-CHESTNUT FAMILY   HIPPOCASTANACEAE

Horse-chestnut   ### Aesculus hippocastanum   (AP 125)

The 'conker' tree. Flowers white (or pink) in 'candles'. The leaves are divided into leaflets, (like the fingers of a hand). Fruits (seeds and their cases) are the conkers.
Height - 20 metres

THE MAPLE FAMILY   ACERACEAE

Deciduous trees, with opposite leaves. Flowers green/yellow in clusters. The seed pod is the two-bladed 'helicopter'.

Field Maple   ### Acer campestre (AP 126)

The wings of the seed pods are almost straight. Leaves with 3 to 5 lobes, barely toothed, often reddish, 6 cms long. Flower clusters stand erect. Common in hedgerows.
Height - 20 metres

Smooth Japanese-maple   ### Acer palmatum (AP 126)

Flowers in erect clusters. Leaves very deeply cut. "Blades" of the seed pods form a very shallow V. *Height - 6 metres*

THE MAPLE FAMILY Cont'd....

Sycamore   Acer pseudoplatanus   (AP 126)

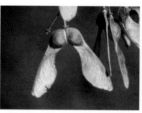

Flowers in drooping bunches. Seed pods with large "blades" which meet at a sharp angle. Leaves large (15 cms) and palmate. *Height - 30 metres*

Norway Maple   Acer platanoides   (AP 125)

Leaves with sharply toothed lobes.
Flower clusters held erect.
Height - 10 cms

Seed pods has large wings (10 cms across). They form an almost straight line.

THE STAGHORN FAMILY   ANACARDIACEAE

Only one member of this Family is recorded.

Stag's-horn Sumach   Rhus hirta   (AP 126)

Leaves pinnate with soft hairs. Soon show
Autumn colouring. Female flowers form dense red head;
male flowers form greenish cluster.
Height - 7 metres

THE OXALIS FAMILY   OXALIDACEAE

Small herbaceous plants. The flowers have five petals and the leaf is divided into three leaflets.

Procumbent Yellow-sorrel   **Oxalis corniculata (AP 126)**

Yellow flowers. Creeping stems which root along their length.
Leaves alternate and sometimes purple. A common weed on lawns. *Height - 50 cms*

Upright Yellow-sorrel   **Oxalis stricta (AP 127)**

A rare garden weed. Very similar to Procumbent Yellow-sorrel but has erect stems (up to 25 cms). The flowers are yellow but only rarely do the leaves show red.

Wood Sorrel   **Oxalis acetosella (AP 127)**

Solitary white flowers, bell shaped. Petals show darker pink/purple veins.
Stems low and creeping. Woodland species. *Height - 10 cms*

THE OXALIS FAMILY Cont'd...

Pink-sorrel

Oxalis articulata   (AP 127)

Leaflets in threes with orange warts on the underside. Flowers deep pink. Stem is a swollen rhizome covered in brown scales,usually just below ground level.
Height - 30 cms

Garden Pink-sorrel

Oxalis latifolia   (AP 127)

Flowers commonly pale pink but sometimes white.

Stem is a rhizome, often ground level and with outgrowing bulbils. Leaflets in threes but without warts.

Pale Pink-sorrel

Oxalis incarnata   (AP 127)

This is a rare introduction which sometimes appears as a garden weed, especially in the west of the County. It is distinguished by the fact that the flowers are held singly and have darker pink veins. The underside of the leaf is unspotted.

THE CRANE'S-BILL & STORK'S-BILL FAMILY   GERANIACEAE

Both have fruits with
a long beak or bill.
Crane's-bills have palmate,
lobed leaves. Stork's-bills
have pinnate leaves.

Meadow Crane's-bill   Geranium pratense (AP 128)

Flowers, large (30 mms)
and blue. Main stem
branches to produce a
cluster of side stems.
Each side stem has a
single flower.
Leaves deeply divided.

Height - 80 cms

Pencilled Crane's-bill   Geranium versicolor (AP 128)

Petals pale pink and
with dark purple 'pencil
marked' veins. Flowers
single. Leaves lobed and
toothed and often with
brown patches.

Height - 60 cms

Dusky Crane's-bill   Geranium phaeum (AP 130)

Petals dark purple with
pale centre. Petals have
small point at their tip and
present a flat face. Flowers
in pairs. Leaves deeply
divided into five
toothed lobes.

Height - 50 cms

THE CRANE'S-BILL & STORK'S-BILL FAMILY Cont'd...

Bloody Crane's-bill

Geranium sanguineum (AP 128)

Petals about 25 mms across and deep purple-red. Flowers single. Leaves deeply divided and grow to form a lowish mat.

Height - 30 cms

Rock Crane's-bill

Geranium macrorrhizum (AP 129)

Flowers in clusters, pale pink petals with dark red sepals. Leaves divided into five toothed lobes.

Height - 50 cms

Knotted Crane's-bill

Geranium nodosum (AP 128)

Flowers pink with deep purple veins. The tip of the bill is a bright red. The leaves are in 3 lobes, and there is a swelling (knotting) where the leaf stalk leaves the stem.

Height - 60 cms

Hedgerow Crane's-bill

Geranium pyrenaicum (AP 129)

Pink flowers (about 15 cms across), in pairs. Petals deeply notched. Rounded leaves divided to about halfway.

Height - 80 cms

Dove's-foot Crane's-bill

Geranium molle (AP 129)

Petals pale pink with a paler centre.
Flowers in pairs. *Height - 40 cms*

Leaves round in outline,
lobed and downy.

Cut-leaved Crane's-bill

Geranium dissectum (AP 129)

Flowers small (less than 10 mms), and
pink. *Height - 60 cms*

Leaves very finely divided.

Long-stalked Crane's-bill

Geranium columbinum (AP 129)

Leaves much divided, but less so than
Cut-leaved form. Flowers on long stalks.
Height - 50 cms

Petals pink with darker veins and sepals
have long points which project beyond
the petals.

Small-flowered Crane's-bill

Geranium pusillum (AP 129)

Small (5 mm) pale pink flowers
with dark veins.

Leaves round in outline, deeply cut.
Height - 30 cms

Shining Crane's-bill

Geranium lucidum (AP 130)

Petals small (10 mms), pink. Leaves very
smooth and shiny.

Plant reddens with age.
Height - 40 cms

Round-leaved Crane's-bill

Geranium rotundifolium (AP 128)

Petals very pale pink, flowers small
(10 mms across).
Height - 40 cms

Leaves divided into lobes but outline is
round. Stems reddish.

THE CRANE'S-BILL & STORK'S-BILL FAMILY Cont'd...

Herb Robert

Geranium robertianum (AP 130)

Petals pink with darker veins and
without notches at the outer edge.
Flowers about 15 mms across.
Leaves much divided, fern like.
Stems and leaves often reddish
and downy.
Height - 50 cms

French Crane's-bill

Flowers large (about 25 mms across) and
bright pink. Petals are pointed at the tip.

Geranium endressii (AP 128)

Leaves lobed and almost star shaped.
Height - 60 cms

THE CRANE'S-BILL & STORK'S-BILL FAMILY Cont'd...

The Stork's-bills can be identified best by examining the type of leaf division.
All have pink flowers.

Common Stork's-bill   **Erodium cicutarium (AP 131)**

Leaves pinnate and leaflets toothed. Has white pointed stipules.
Often has two dark spots at the base of the two larger petals.
Height - 40 cms

Sea Stork's-bill   **Erodium maritimum (AP 130)**

A rare coastal plant. Prostrate, growing from small rosette. Flowers small (5 mms) and
pale pink. Leaves stalked and toothed.
Height - 10 cms

Musk Stork's-bill   **Erodium moschatum (AP 130)**

A sticky, hairy plant. Flowers small (about 2 cms) and in clusters. Leaves toothed but
not finely divided. Taller than the other Stork's-bill.
Height - 30 cms

THE BALSAM FAMILY   **BALSAMINACEAE**

The members of this Family have flowers of a unique shape; the centre is a tube which
opens at the front to form petals and at the rear, the tube narrows to a spur.

Indian Balsam   **Impatiens glandulifera (AP 131)**
Or Himalayan Balsam or Policeman's helmet.

Flowers pink/purple,
occasionally white.
Spur bent.
The ripe seed pod
"explodes" when touched
and the seeds shoot out.
Height - 2 metres

THE IVY FAMILY   ARALIACEAE

Creeping evergreen climber.

Ivy   Hedera helix (AP 132)

Leaves vary in shape; young leaves are often star-shaped but older ones are almost diamond shape. Clusters of small yellow flowers are carried at the end of the year. Fruits are black berries.

Height - several metres depending on support.

THE COW PARSLEY or CARROT FAMILY
APIACEAE
Sometimes called the **UMBELLIFERAE**

This is a large Family. Including rarities etc. the *Atlas* refers to 60+ species. The flowers of the species of this Family are carried on umbels. The umbels are like the spokes of an umbrella. The individual flowers are all very similar, with five petals, often the outer petals are larger. A few are yellow, the majority are white/pinkish. The common names can be misleading in that the various 'parsleys' are not all closely related.

The factors that help in identification are:-

The size, shape and position of the umbels.

The presence (or otherwise) of lower bracts (small leaf-like growths). These are usually pointed and grow out from the base of the umbels, upper bracts are similar but grow out from the base of the secondary umbels.

The shape of the leaves.

The shape of the seed pods.

The growth habit e.g. prostrate, watery habitat etc.

THE COW PARSLEY OR CARROT FAMILY Cont'd...

Those with yellow flowers.

Alexanders   Smyrnium olusatrum (AP 133)

Tall (about 1.5 metres). Leaves divided into three flat lobes. Usually near the coast. Young stems solid becoming hollow with age. *Height - 1.5 metres*

Wild Parsnip   Pastinaca sativa (AP 139)

Leaves pinnate with broad, toothed leaflets.
Umbels usually without bracts. Stem hollow and ridged.
Height - 1.5 metres

Pepper-saxifrage   Silaum silaus (AP 136)

Flower is a very pale yellow with few or no bracts.
Lower leaves pinnate with narrow leaflets. Stem leaves few.
Height - 1 metre

THE COW PARSLEY OR CARROT FAMILY Cont'd...

Rock Samphire

Crithmum maritimum (AP 135)

Thick fleshy leaves. Rigid solid stem. Has short, stubby leaf-like upper and lower bracts. Usually on rocky coastal ground. *Height - 40 cms*

Fennel

Foeniculum vulgare (AP 136)

Leaves long, thin and needle like; leaf stalks flattened.
Has distinctive aniseed smell.
Yellow flowers usually without bracts.
Height - 2.5 metres

Slender Hare's-ear

Bupleurum tenuissimum (AP 137)

Slender stemmed and sprawling. Flowers very small, single umbels. The splash of colour is from the pollen. Leaves few, narrow and pointed. *Height - 40 cms*

THE COW PARSLEY OR CARROT FAMILY Cont'd...

Those with white or pinkish-white flowers.

Plants growing in or near water.

The Water-dropwort group all grow either in or near water. They are hairless perennials. The leaves are pinnate and much divided with pointed leaflets. The leaf stalks are flattened and wrap around the stem for part of their length.

Tubular Water-dropwort   **Oenanthe fistulosa   (AP 135)**

Upright habitat. Grey/green leaves with a few pairs of narrow, rolled leaflets. Small umbels with upper bracts. Grows in water. Stem hollow.
Height - 30 cms above water level.

Fine-leaved Water-dropwort   **Oenanthe aquatica   (AP 136)**

Submerged leaves with very fine leaflets. Aerial leaves pinnate forming narrow triangular outline. Umbel with upper and lower bracts. Stem hollow.
Height - 1 metre

River Water-dropwort   **Oenanthe fluviatilis   (AP 136)**

A rare Water-dropwort occurring in slow moving rivers, e.g. River Cary. It is fully submerged in early Spring with very narrow leaflets. Aerial fan shaped leaves appear in Summer, along with the flowers. The umbels have upper bracts.
Height - 1.5 metres

Parsley Water-dropwort

Oenanthe lachenalii   (AP 135)

Flower umbels have small upper bracts and more noticeable lower ones. Leaflets are long and slender. Stem solid. *Height - 1 metre*

Hemlock Water-dropwort

Oenanthe crocata   (AP 135)

Tall (1.5 metres) and bushy. Leaves flatly pinnate. Umbel with upper and lower bracts. Stem hollow. *Height - 1.5 metres*

Corky-fruited Water-dropwort

Oenanthe pimpinelloides   (AP 135)

Flowers often have pink tinge, with often unequal length lower bracts. Upper leaves few, long and slender. Lower leaves pinnate. Stubby lower bracts present.

Height - 1 metre

THE COW PARSLEY OR CARROT FAMILY Cont'd...

Marsh Pennywort   Hydrocotyle vulgaris   (AP 132)

Prostrate low-growing. Round leaves with scalloped edges. Leaf stalk is in centre of the leaf. No bracts. Flowers rare and very small (2 mms). *Height - 10 cms*

Lesser Marshwort   Apium inundatum   (AP 138)

Mostly underwater and sprawling. Submerged leaves very finely divided, aerial ones with narrow leaflets. Small umbels with upper bracts only.
Height - 50 cms (sprawling).

Angelica   Angelica sylvestris   (AP 139)

Tall (2 metres). Leaves pinnate; the outermost tips of the leaves forming an equilateral triangle. No bracts. Umbels dome-shaped and pinkish. Lives near, but not usually in water. *Height - 2 metres*

THE COW PARSLEY OR CARROT FAMILY Cont'd...

Fool's Water-cress

Apium nodiflorum (AP 138)

Grows in water. Pinnate leaves with large toothed leaflets; three to six pairs of leaflets. Sprawling growth. Flower stalk grows side-ways from a leaf joint rather than at the tip of the stem. Umbels small and well separated from each other. No lower bracts. *Height - 60 cms*

Greater Water-parsnip

Sium latifolium (AP 134)

A very rare plant. Tall (1.5 metres). Pinnate leaves, leaflets large, oval and finely toothed. Occasionally lower submerged leaves. Umbels held well above rest of plant. Large lower bracts. Stem hollow. Usually on edge of a ditch. *Height - 1.5 metres*

Lesser Water-parsnip

Berula erecta (AP 134)

Usually in water, with some aerial stems and flowers. Sprawling. Upper leaves fern like with about ten toothed leaflets. Has both upper and lower bracts; the bracts usually forked. *Height - 50 cms*

THE COW PARSLEY OR CARROT FAMILY Cont'd...

Milk Parsley   Peucedanum palustre   (AP 139)

Usually in alkaline soil. Grows slightly higher than the surrounding vegetation. Leaves divided and triangular in outline. Upper and lower bracts.
Height - 1.5 metres

Members of the Family with white flowers not usually found in or near water and in a restricted habitat.

Honewort   Trinia glauca   (AP 137)

Usually on dry limestone grassland. Low sprawling growth; solid stem. Greyish pinnate leaves, leaves narrow. Base of leaf stalk flattened. Umbels with lower bracts either absent or only 1 or 2; upper bracts very few. *Height - 20 cms*

Sanicle   Sanicula europaea   (AP 132)

Usually in woodland habitats. Leaves palmate, lobes toothed. Umbels separate and in small tight heads. Hairless. Has upper and lower bracts.

Height - 50 cms

THE COW PARSLEY OR CARROT FAMILY Cont'd...

The rest of this Family can be described either as wayside plants or introductions. Their identification often depends on more than one single characteristic. They all have white flowers.

Astrantia

Astrantia major   (AP 132)

Flowers in tight head with outer bracts giving ruff-like appearance. Leaves palmate, deeply lobed and sharply toothed. Erect hairless stem.

Height - 75 cms

Shepherd's-needle

Height - 50 cms

Scandix pecten-veneris   (AP 133)

Lower leaves much divided but almost round in outline. Hairless. Seed pods like a bunch of up-stretched fingers (or needles).

Hemlock

Conium maculatum   (AP 137)

One of only two of this Family with stems splashed with red/purple marks. Hollow stem. Leaves light green and pinnate. Has upper and lower bracts. Very poisonous.

Height - 2 metres

THE COW PARSLEY OR CARROT FAMILY Cont'd...

Rough Chervil   Chaerophyllum temulum (AP 132)

The only other member of the family with a stem with purple markings. Coarsely hairy with solid stem. Leaves pinnate, narrow triangular in outline. Umbel with upper bracts only. Flowers later than Cow Parsley. Much smaller and more delicate than Hemlock.
Height - 1 metre

Corn Parsley   Petroselinum segetum (AP 138)

Has very small umbels. Slender, hairless, solid stem. Smells of Parsley. Lower leaves pinnate upper leaves long and Narrow. Upper and lower bracts also long and narrow.

Height - 1 metre

Stone Parsley   Sison amomum (AP 138)

Has small umbels with few rays. Solid, wiry stem. Smells of petrol.

Bristle-like upper bracts.; lower bracts very small.

Leaves pinnate with very narrow leaflets.
Height - 1.5 metres

THE COW PARSLEY OR CARROT FAMILY Cont'd...

Hogweed   Heracleum sphondylium (AP 139)

Coarse, roughly hairy plant. Leaves pinnate with broad toothed leaflets. Hollow, ridged stem. Umbels with many rays, soon look dusty. Usually narrow lower bracts.
Height - 1.5 metres

Giant Hogweed   Heracleum mantegazzianum (AP 140)

Very large; umbels up to 50 cms across. Leaves large with sharply pointed leaflets. Short bracts below the umbels. Stem hollow and ridged.

Height - 4 metres

Spreading Hedge-parsley   Torilis arvensis (AP 140)

Low growing (40 cms), grey/green. Umbels long-stalked on wiry stems.
Lower bracts either absent or very few. *Height - 40 cms*

THE COW PARSLEY OR CARROT FAMILY Cont'd...

Knotted Hedge-parsley

Torilis nodosa (AP 140)

Low growing (40 cms). Rough, hairy and sprawling. Umbel stalk very short. Umbels roughly spherical and close to stem. Long thin upper bracts which spread beyond the flowers. *Height - 40 cms*

Wild Carrot

Daucus carota (AP 140)

Young umbels are convex but they become concave as they mature. Forked bracts which form a ruff round the umbel. Stems solid and roughly hairy. Leaves pinnate and feathery. *Height - 80 cms*

The next two species both have prominent upper and lower bracts and solid stem.

Bullwort

Ammi majus (AP 138)

Solid stem. Umbels with long branched bracts. *Height - 1 metre*

Leaves grey-green and pinnate; the leaflets with pointed teeth.

THE COW PARSLEY OR CARROT FAMILY Cont'd...

Upright Hedge-parsley   Torilis japonica (AP 140)

Solid stem. Umbels with upper and lower bracts.
Leaves broadly pinnate.
Height - 1.5 metres

Ground-elder   Aegopodium podagraria (AP 134)

Creeping, hollow hairless stems,
which put out upright aerial shoots.
Flower heads without bracts.
Leaves pinnate with heart-shaped toothed
leaflets. *Height - 50 cms*

Wild Celery   Apium graveolens (AP 137)

Neither upper nor lower bracts. Solid stem, smells of celery. Umbel stalks vary in length
giving a loose head. Leaves with broad toothed leaflets. *Height - 1 metre*

THE COW PARSLEY OR CARROT FAMILY Cont'd...

Fool's Parsley   **Aethusa cynapium (AP 136)**

Umbel has very long upper bracts which project well below the umbel.
No lower bracts. Hairless. Leaves pinnate.
Height - 1 metre

Burnet-saxifrage   **Pimpinella saxifraga (AP 134)**

Not a saxifrage. Of the remaining species, the only one with
a solid stem. No lower bracts, upper bracts present.
Leaves pinnate, leaflets rounded and toothed.
Leaf stalks flattened. *Height - 60 cms*

Garden Angelica   **Angelica archangelica (AP 139)**

Umbels greeny-white. Upper bracts present, lower bracts none or very short-lived.
Leaf stalks flattened. Leaves with few broad-toothed irregular leaflets. Stem hollow.
Height - 1.5 metres

THE COW PARSLEY OR CARROT FAMILY Cont'd...

Of the remaining four species, two are covered in downy hairs.

<u>Cow Parsley</u>   <u>Anthriscus sylvestris</u> **(AP 133)**

Very common. Shows in early Spring as bright green leaves. Stem later turns purple. Downy hollow stems. Umbel without lower bracts. Seed pods are a slim oval shape.
Height - 1 metre

<u>Sweet Cicely</u>   <u>Myrrhis odorata</u> **(AP 133)**

Umbels close together. No lower bracts, upper bracts narrow and pointed. Aromatic, with downy hairs. Leaves feathery and with flattened leaf stalks. Long narrow pods.
Height - 1 metre

The remaining two species have hollow, smooth stems.

<u>Pignut</u>   <u>Conopodium majus</u> **(AP 134)**

Woodland species, not very tall (40 cms). Umbels form an open spray. No lower bracts; few upper bracts. Smooth hollow stem. Leaves divided into narrow leaflets, each with hairy edge. *Height - 40 cms*

THE COW PARSLEY OR CARROT FAMILY Cont'd...

Bur Parsley
Sometimes Bur Chervil   **Anthriscus caucalis   (AP 133)**

Often on sandy soils near the coast. Smooth hollow stem. Flower clusters very small and umbels form a loose spray. No lower bracts; upper bracts fringed. Leaves finely divided. Seed pods have red burs. *Height - 60 cms*

THE GENTIAN FAMILY   GENTIANACEAE

The petals form a tube which opens out to show the five or six separate petals. Sepals are long and thin. Leaves simple, opposite each other and in some species, stalkless.

Yellow-wort   **Blackstonia perfoliata (AP 141)**

Yellow petals fused at base. Leaves grey-green fused in pairs across the stem. Flowers form a loose head. *Height - 30 cms*

THE GENTIAN FAMILY Cont'd...

Common Centaury   Centaurium erythraea (AP 141)

Flowers, with short stalks form a loose cluster.
Has a basal rosette of leaves. Five pink petals, tubular at
base. Stem leaves have three veins.
Height - 30 cms

Lesser Centaury   Centaurium pulchellum (AP 141)

Flowers on stems which branch frequently.
Sepals longer than the flower stalks.
No basal rosette. Five pink petals
which open from the tube to give a
star-like pattern.
Height - 12 cms

Early Gentian   Gentianella anglica (AP 142)

Autumn Gentian (Felwort)   Gentianella amarella (AP 141)

Two very similar (and rare) flowers. Both have purple-red flowers in dense clusters.
As their name implies they flower at different seasons.
Early Gentian is smaller (up to 12cms) whilst the Autumn Gentian grows up to 25 cms).

Early Gentian

The flowers usually have four petals and
short sepals. Autumn Gentian usually has
five petals and longer sepals.
Height - 3-12 cms

213

THE PERIWINKLE FAMILY   APOCYNACEAE

The *Atlas* refers to three species. One is Intermediate Periwinkle which is recorded from only one small site. The other two species are shown below. They are scrambling plants. Simple leaves arranged opposite each other. Flowers with five petals which look slightly 'off centre'.

Greater Periwinkle   Vinca major (AP 142)

Large (4 cms across) 5-petalled blue flowers. Sepals long and thin. Leaves opposite in pairs; sometimes variegated. Some stems prostrate and rooting at intervals.
Height - length - 1 metre

Lesser Periwinkle   Vinca minor (AP 142)

Smaller (2 cms across) 5-petalled purple flowers. Petals 'off centre'. Sepals short. Leaves opposite in pairs on very short stalks. Stems nearly all prostrate. *Height - length - 60 cms*

THE NIGHTSHADE FAMILY   SOLANACEAE

Plants with five petals, often joined at the base. Five sepals. Unstalked alternate leaves. Although this Family includes potatoes and tomatoes, it is best to treat all the wild forms as very poisonous.

Thorn-apple   Datura stramonium (AP 144)

Large (6 cms) white petals, trumpet-shaped and pointed at the tip. Large thorny "fruits", the sepals remain as a green collar. Leaves large and strongly toothed. *Height - 1 metre*

Henbane   Hyoscyamus niger (AP 143)

Flowers have yellow/cream petals with dark markings. Anthers are purple. Leaves sharply toothed. Fruit is a green berry inside the sepals. Sepals green, hairy, drying to brown, flask-shaped. *Height - 70 cms*

Apple of Peru   Nicandra physalodes (AP 142)

Flowers (3 cms) bell-shaped; pale - purple colour. Sepals large and bladder-like. Leaves pointedly toothed. Fruit is straw-coloured berry held in the sepals. *Height - 1 metre*

Deadly Nightshade

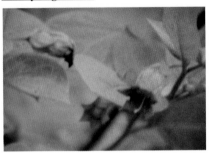

Flowers a dull purple, bell-shaped,
(3 cms across). Leaves broadly pointed,
oval. Fruit a shiny black berry.
Height - 1.5 metres

Atropa belladonna (AP 143)

Bittersweet

Purple petals with yellow anthers, sepals
and stalk purplish. Sprawling climber,
old stem becomes woody.

Solanum dulcamara (AP 144)

Fruit ripens to a red berry.
Height - 2 metres

THE NIGHTSHADE FAMILY Cont'd....

Black Nightshade

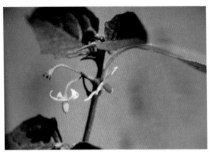

Small white flowers with yellow anthers.
Stem dark, leaves oval.

Solanum nigrum (AP 143)

Berries become black on ripening.
Height - 50 cms

Duke of Argyll's Teaplant

Lycium barbarum (AP 142)

Long, arching stems. Pale purple flowers with yellow anthers. Five petals joined for
about half their length. Leaves long and narrow, broadest across the centre and
arranged alternately.
Height - 2.5 metres

Chinese Teaplant

Similar to Duke of Argyll's but petals
divided to more than half way.

Lycium chinense (AP 143)

Leaves broadest near the base.
Height - 4 metres

THE BINDWEED FAMILY   CONVOLVULACEAE

Flowers large and trumpet shaped, white or pink petals. Flowers have five petals and five sepals. Stems climb by twining. Leaves alternate and heart-shaped.

Field Bindweed

Flowers white with pink outer edges; about 2 cms across. Forms mats at roadside.

Convolvulus arvensis   (AP 144)

Leaves blunt arrow-head shape.
Height - when climbing, 1 metre

Sea Bindweed

Calystegia soldanella   (AP 145)

Flowers pink with white stripes, about 3-4 cms across. Leaves fleshy and roundly heart-shaped. Sprawls along the ground, particularly on dunes.
Height - 5 cms Sprawls at ground level up to 1 metre.

Hedge Bindweed

Calystegia sepium   (AP 145)

Flowers large (4 cms across) and white. Five sepals half covered by two large bracts. *Height - 2 metres*

Large Bindweed

Calystegia silvatica   (AP 145)

Flowers large (6 cms across) and white. Sepals covered completely by two large bracts.
Height - 3 metres

Hairy Bindweed

Calystegia pulchra   (AP 145)

A rare species which has probably been introduced to a few sites.
Very like Large Bindweed but downy. Petals are pink with white stripes.
Height - 2.5 metres

THE DODDER FAMILY   CUSCUTACEAE

Parasitic plants without roots. Plant consists of intertwining red stems and tight heads of very small flowers.

Dodder   Cuscuta epithymum (AP 145)

Thread like stem, usually on Gorse or Heather. Leaves reduced to tiny scales. Flowers pink, bell-shaped with long stamens, in clusters. *Height - as host plant*

THE BOGBEAN FAMILY   MENYANTHACEAE

Two aquatic plants; flowers with five fringed petals.

Creeping aquatic with leaves a little like those of a Broad Bean. Petals white on the inside and pink on the outside. Petals fringed. Flowers on a spike.
Height above water - 20 cms

THE BOGBEAN FAMILY Cont'd....

Fringed Water-lily   ### Nymphoides peltata (AP 146)

Creeping aquatic with leaves floating on water surface. Flowers with five yellow petals.
Petals each have a more intense yellow triangle in the centre. Petals fringed.
Height above water - 10 cms

THE FORGET-ME-NOT
or THE COMFREY FAMILY   ## BORAGINACEAE

Leaves and stem bristly hairy. Flowers on curved stems, sometimes straightening at
maturity. Five petals and five sepals, each often fused at the base to form a tube.

For identification purposes it is probably easier to take the Forget-me-not group first.

Forget-me-nots   ### Myosotis species

Flowers small and usually pale blue
but sometimes pink especially in bud.
Flowers on drooping spikes.
Leaves bristly, long, narrow and oval.

Changing Forget-me-not   ### Myosotis discolor (AP 150)

Stem with coiled tip.
Flowers yellow at first,
changing to blue with age.
Sepals are longer than the
flower stalk but shorter
than the petal tube and
have hooked hairs.
Height - 15 cms

THE FORGET-ME-NOT FAMILY Cont'd....

Water Forget-me-not   **Myosotis scorpioides (AP 149)**

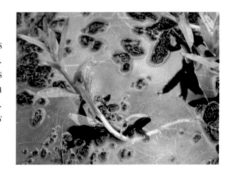

Larger (5 cms), pale green leaves
and growing in or near water.
Flowers bright blue and about 10 mms
across. Has creeping runners which
usually run just below the water surface.
Height - 50 cms

Tufted Forget-me-not   **Myosotis laxa   (AP 149)**

A smaller version of Water Forget-me-not (flowers about 4 mms across).
No creeping runners. Also grows in or near water. *Height - 40 cms*

Creeping Forget-me-not   **Myosotis secunda   (AP 149)**

Grows in wet, usually acidic soil.
Creeping habit.
Height - 6 cms

Flowers small, about 6 mms across.
Sepals fused for half their length.

222

THE FORGET-ME-NOT FAMILY Cont'd....

Early Forget-me-not

Flowers very small (2-3 mms across).
Leaves mostly in basal rosette.
Height - 20 cms

Myosotis ramosissima (AP 150)

Dark sepals protrude beyond the petal tube.

Wood Forget-me-not

Myosotis sylvatica (AP 150)

Flowers clear blue and about 8 mms across. Open part of the petals is longer than the tube. Sepals as long as the petal tube. Relatively large (5 cms) leaves.
Height - 40 cms

Field Forget-me-not

Plant is a grey-green. Flowers small (4 mms across) and blue-grey.
Height - 30 cms

Myosotis arvensis (AP 150)

The petal tube is enclosed in a ring of bristly hairy sepals.

THE FORGET-ME-NOT FAMILY Cont'd....

Similar species other than Forget-me-nots.

Usually larger, coarser and bristly-hairy. Two species are very similar to Forget-me-nots.

Blue-eyed-Mary

Omphalodes verna (AP 150)

Prostrate stem forming open mat. Flowers bright blue and about 12 mms across, white stamens. Leaves pointed oval. *Height - 20 cms*

Great Forget-me-not

Brunnera macrophylla (AP 148)

Leaves heart-shaped and lower ones have long leaf stalk. Leaves have coarse appearance. Flowers in clusters; small about 4 mms across and pale-blue. *Height - 40 cms*

Six members of this group have flowers mainly blue but often also have some pink/red petals.

Lungwort

Pulmonaria officinalis (AP 147)

The shortest in this section. (25 cms). Leaves rough, narrowly pointed and with white blotches. Flowers start pink and turn purple with age. *Height - 25 cms*

224

THE FORGET-ME-NOT FAMILY Cont'd....

Bugloss

Anchusa arvensis (AP 148)

Has small (4 mms across) pale blue flowers. *Height - 40 cms*

Leaves very bristly, wavy edged, narrow and long.

Borage

Borago officinalis (AP 149)

Petals very bright blue and open to a pointed star. Petals often bend backwards. Flowers in clusters with flower stalks and sepals reddish; covered in white hairs.

Leaves oval and coarsely bristled. *Height - 60 cms*

Green Alkanet

Pentaglottis sempervirens (AP 149)

Flowers deep blue with a white centre. Petal edges rounded. *Height - 1 metre*

Whole plant covered in stiff white hairs. Leaves oval and toothed.

THE FORGET-ME-NOT FAMILY Cont'd....

Viper's-bugloss

Echium vulgare (AP 147)

Height - 80 cms

Plants often grow in clumps of spires. Flowers pink in bud, opening to blue with long styles. Leaves long and narrow. Plant covered in red bristly hairs. Common on sandy soils, especially sand dunes.

Abraham-Isaac-Jacob

Trachystemon orientalis (AP 149)

Creeping plant with rough hairs. Leaves heart-shaped with long stalk.
Flowers in a drooping cluster. Purple petals fold back to show long purple stamens.
Height - 30 cms

These are two species whose flowers are predominately purple.

Purple Gromwell

Lithospermum purpurocaeruleum (AP 146)

Leaves long and narrow with short stalks and downy hairs. Flowers red/purple, turning blue with age. Petals open into five-petalled stars. *Height - 50 cms*

THE FORGET-ME-NOT FAMILY Cont'd….

<u>Hound's-tongue</u> <u>Cynoglossum officinale</u> (AP 150)

Grey-green plant with downy hairs and narrow oval leaves. Petals held by sepals into a cup-shape. Flowers red and purple on a spike. Seed head of four flattened spiny looking "pods". *Height - 60 cms*

Members of the group with white or purple petals.

<u>Common Comfrey</u> <u>Symphytum officinale</u> (AP 147)

The whole plant coarsely hairy. The flower colour varies from creamy-white to bluish purple. Sepals long and pointed and as long as petal tube. Stem winged. Lower leaves broad oval, upper leaves narrow. Usually in damp habitat.

Height - 1.2 metres

Members of the group with white/cream flowers.

<u>White Comfrey</u> <u>Symphytum orientale</u> (AP 148)

Flowers pure white. Sepals short and blunt. Stem leaves broad oval with pointed tip. *Height - 60 cms*

THE FORGET-ME-NOT FAMILY Cont'd....

Tuberous Comfrey

Flowers yellow-cream turning brown at the tip.
Height - 60 cms

Symphytum tuberosum (AP 148)

Sepal long and narrow. Usually in damp habitats.

Creeping Comfrey

Patch forming. Flower buds with reddish tips, maturing to yellow-cream.

Symphytum grandiflorum (AP 148)

Sepals long and thin.
Height - 20 cms

Field Gromwell (Corn Cromwell)

Lithospermum arvense (AP 147)

Stem scarcely branched. Small (3 mms) flowers in short clusters. Petal tube sometimes purple when very young. Leaves long and narrow.
Height - 50 cms

THE FORGET-ME-NOT FAMILY Cont'd....

Common Gromwell   **Lithospermum officinale (AP 146)**

Erect, much branched. Leaves long and roughly hairy. Flowers small (3 mms) greenish white. Flowers in small dense clusters. *Height - 60 cms*

THE VERBENA FAMILY   VERBENACEAE

The *Atlas* records only one member of this Family.

Vervain   **Verbena officinalis (AP 151)**

Flowers small (5 mms) pink/lilac and on tall spikes. Leaves few and deeply cut. Petal tube divides into two lobed lower lips and three upper ones. Sepals about half the length of the petal tube. *Height - 70 cms*

THE DEAD NETTLE FAMILY   LAMIACEAE (LABIATES)

The petals open from a   tube to form an upper hood and lower landing stage. There are five sepals.

THE DEAD-NETTLE FAMILY Cont'd....

Some members of the Family can be identified by their distinct petal colour.

Plants with yellow petals.

<u>**Yellow Archangel**</u>   <u>**Lamiastrum galeobdolon**</u> **(AP 152)**

Large yellow flowers, sometimes with red markings. Landing petal with 3 lobes; large hood petal. Long leafy runners. Usually in woodlands. *Height - 40 cms*

<u>**Wood Sage**</u>   <u>**Teucrium scorodonia**</u>   **(AP 154)**

Creamy-yellow flowers in pairs on stiff, upright stems. Purple anthers. Leaves oval toothed and downy. Flowers in long slender spikes. *Height - 60 cms*

Plants with mainly white petals.

<u>**White Dead-nettle**</u>   <u>**Lamium album**</u>   **(AP 152)**

Large (20 mms) white flowers with open 'mouth'. Landing petals made up of two large outer sections and a smaller triangular central one. Four black anthers under the large hood petal. Leaves heart-shaped and toothed. They do not sting. *Height - 60 cms*

THE DEAD-NETTLE FAMILY Cont'd....

<u>Bastard Balm</u>   **<u>Melittis melissophyllum (AP 154)</u>**

Flowers large (30 mms) and in clusters along the stem. Sepals short. Leaves pointed oval and toothed. Petals white but with variable pink markings.
Height - 60 cms

<u>Balm</u>   **<u>Melissa officinalis (AP 156)</u>**

Small (8 mms) white flowers in clusters along the stem.
Leaves toothed, oval and lemon scented. *Height - 80 cms*

<u>Cat-mint</u>   **<u>Nepeta cataria (AP 155)</u>**

Flowers white with purple spots in compact heads. Plant grey and downy.
Clump forming. *Height - 30 cms*

THE DEAD-NETTLE FAMILY Cont'd....

Cut-leaved Selfheal

Dry limey habitat. White flowers in tight head.

Prunella laciniata (AP 155)

Stem and pinnate leaves downy.
Height - 25 cms

White Horehound

White flowers in whorls. Hood petal divided into two.

Marrubium vulgare (AP 154)

Leaves and stem grey with woolly down. Petals go brown with age. *Height - 50cms*

Four species have flowers which are blue

Bugle

Ajuga reptans (AP 155)

Low growing, with short (20 cms) spires of whorls of blue flowers. Aerial stems have rows of hairs on opposite sides. Leaves oval, lobed and often purplish. Prostrate stem roots at intervals. *Height - 25 cms*

THE DEAD-NETTLE FAMILY Cont'd....

Rosemary

A shrub. Flowers a dusty blue.
Height - 2 metres

Skullcap

Rosmarinus officinalis (AP 159)

Needle-shaped leaves with a distinctive scent.

Scutellaria galericulata (AP 154)

Sprawling growth. Leaves unstalked, narrow, heart-shaped and toothed. Flowers blue and in pairs. Lower lip protrudes like a tongue and has a pale centre with dark markings.
Height - 40 cms

Flowers in the pink-red-purple range

Not all the petals in the same flower are the same shade. Some change colour as they age.

This group can be further divided: -
Mints with distinctive taste/aroma.
Low growing plants with prostrate stems that give short spikes of flowers.
Those that produce tallish upright stems.

THE DEAD-NETTLE FAMILY Cont'd….

Mints

Strongly scented. Flowers pale purple in tight whorls.

Water Mint   **Mentha aquatica (AP 158)**

Waterside plant. Stems prostrate and rooting, often under water. Sweetish scent.
Leaves hairy toothed and stalkless. Flower heads large and round and often with a
second head below. *Height - 30 cms above water.*

Pennyroyal   **Mentha pulegium (AP 159)**

Sprawling and
downy. Flowers
in whorls.
Often prostrate
stem. Leaves
small, oval and
pointed.

Height - 25 cms

Round-leaved mint   **Mentha suaveolens (AP 158)**

Soft, downy
plant. Flowers
on branched
spikes.
Leaves round.

Height - 50 cms

THE DEAD-NETTLE FAMILY Cont'd….

Spearmint

Mentha spicata   (AP 158)

Garden mint. Hairless, flowers in terminal spires.

Leaves narrow, pointed and toothed.
Height - 50 cms

Corn Mint

Mentha arvensis   (AP 157)

Flowers in separate whorls up the stem. Aromatic. Leaves oval, pointed and toothed.

Height - 60 cms

Low growing members of this Family with pink/purplish flower.

Ground-ivy

Glechoma hederacea   (AP 155)

Long creeping and rooting runners; mat forming. Flowers purple. Petals form a longish tube which opens into 5 lobes. Leaves roundish and toothed.
Height - 20 cms

THE DEAD-NETTLE FAMILY Cont'd....

Selfheal   Prunella vulgaris (AP 155)

Low creeping runners. Lower leaves pointed oval, upper leaves thinner and almost stalkless. Flowers strong violet/purple in compact head. *Height - 20 cms*

Spotted Dead-nettle   Lamium maculatum (AP 153)

Low, sprawling growth; stems sometimes rooting along their length. Leaves sometimes variegated, toothed, pointed and oval. Flowers pink; petals have wide 'mouth'. *Height - 25 cms*

Red Dead-nettle   Lamium purpureum (AP 153)

Low growing and often branching to put out a clump of vertical stems. Stems and leaves often reddish. Flowers reddish-pink. Leaves round, toothed and stalked. *Height - 20 cms*

Cut-leaved Dead-nettle   Lamium hybridum (AP 153)

An uncommon plant much like Red Dead-nettle but individual flowers have shorter petal tubes making it look very compact. Leaves deeply toothed. *Height - 20 cms*

THE DEAD-NETTLE FAMILY Cont'd....

Lesser Skullcap

Scutellaria minor (AP 154)

Weak short stem. Lower leaves with few teeth, upper leaves long and thin.
Flowers in pairs. Petals pale pink with a longish tube. *Height - 15 cms*

Wall Germander

Teucrium chamaedrys (AP 155)

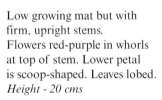

Low growing mat but with
firm, upright stems.
Flowers red-purple in whorls
at top of stem. Lower petal
is scoop-shaped. Leaves lobed.
Height - 20 cms

Basil Thyme

Clinopodium acinos (AP 156)

Low prostrate plant. Flowers violet with white patch on lower lip.
Leaves round and slightly toothed. *Height - 20 cms*

THE DEAD-NETTLE FAMILY Cont'd....

Wild Thyme

Thymus polytrichus (AP 157)

Aromatic. Very low growing (less than 10 cms). Shrubby mat forming.
Height - 10 cms

Flowering stem erect with pink-purple round compact heads of flowers. Stem has hairs on opposing sides.

Large Thyme

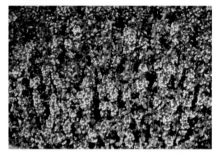

Thymus pulegioides (AP 157)

Shrubby, no creeping runners. Very aromatic. Flowers in pink-purple heads which stand up above the mat of leaves. Stem has hairs on the angles.
Height - 20 cms

THE DEAD-NETTLE FAMILY Cont'd....

The remaining species all have more or less upright stems and flowers in the pink/purple range.

Lamb's-ear

Stachys byzantina (AP 151)

Small bushy plant covered in dense whitish down. Pink flowers in whorls.
A garden escape. *Height - 50 cms*

Gipsywort

Lycopus europaeus (AP 157)

Leaves deeply toothed. Usually near water. Small flowers in whorls. Flowers very pale
pink with purple dots. *Height - 50 cms*

Wild Basil

Clinopodium vulgare (AP 156)

Leaves stalkless, oval and bluntly toothed. Pale pink flowers in whorls.
Height - 60 cms

THE DEAD-NETTLE FAMILY Cont'd....

Betony

Stachys officinalis   (AP 151)

Leaves narrow-oval and bluntly toothed.
Bright pink-purple flowers in compact head at the top of the stem.
Height - 50 cms

Wild Clary

Salvia verbenaca   (AP 159)

Flowers blue-purple with wide 'mouth' and large hood; but not always opening.
Leaves bluntly lobed. Sepals with long narrow points; hairy.
Height - 60 cms

Henbit Dead-nettle

Lamium amplexicaule   (AP 153)

Flowers purple with long paler tube. Leaves round and bluntly toothed.
Most of the flowers at the top of stem. *Height - 50 cms*

THE DEAD-NETTLE FAMILY Cont'd....

Wild Marjoram

Origanum vulgare (AP 156)

Reddish stem branching near the top to give head of pinkish flowers. Aromatic. Leaves small, oval and very slightly toothed.

Height - 50 cms

Common Calamint

Clinopodium ascendens (AP 156)

Flowers in loose, whorls; pink with dark spots.
Leaves have a strong smell of mint and are broad-oval, toothed.
Height - 50 cms

Black Horehound

Ballota nigra (AP 152)

Greyish-green plant. Pinkish/purple flowers in whorls. Occasionally petals are absent.
When petals are present they look like open jaws. Leaves stalkless, toothed and oval.
Height - 75 cms

THE DEAD-NETTLE FAMILY Cont'd….

Common Hemp-nettle   Galeopsis tetrahit (AP 153)

Whorls of pinkish flowers with darker markings on lower lip.
Sepals long and needle like. Leaves greyish green, long narrow and toothed.
Height - 50 cms

Bifid Hemp-nettle   Galeopsis bifida (AP 154)

A scarce plant, similar to Common Hemp-nettle but darker and with more extensive
dark markings on petals.
Height - 50 cms

Hedge Woundwort   Stachys sylvatica (AP 151)

Whorls of dark purple-red flowers. White markings, especially on lower lip.
Lower leaves stalked, heart-shaped and toothed. Plant rough and hairy.
Height - 80 cms

242

THE DEAD-NETTLE FAMILY Cont'd....

Marsh Woundwort   Stachys palustris   (AP 151)

Whorls of pinkish purple
flowers. Flowers have both white
and dark red/purple markings.
Leaves stalkless, pointed-ovals
Plant softly hairy.
Height - 60 cms

Field Woundwort   Stachys arvensis   (AP 152)

Flowers pale pink. Smaller (20 cms) than the other Woundworts.
Leaves stalkless, oval and toothed. *Height - 20 cms*

THE MARE'S-TAIL FAMILY   HIPPURIDACEAE

Only one member of this Family is recorded. It should not be confused with Horsetails;
Horsetails have neither flowers nor true leaves.

Mare's-tail   Hippuris vulgaris   (AP 159)

Grows in water with much
of the stem submerged.
Aerial part of stem has
whorls of long, narrow,
dark-green leaves. Flowers
are pink but insignificant.

Height above water - 25 cms

THE WATER-STARWORT FAMILY CALLITRICHACEAE

A very difficult group to identify to species level and perhaps should be left to the experts. The text gives only brief diagnostic features.

Common Water-starwort Callitriche stagnalis (AP 160)

Has submerged narrow, heart-shaped leaves. Floating leaves are broad and form a rosette at the water surface. *Submerged stem - 50+ cms long.*

Other Water-starworts-

Those with long strap-shaped leaves
Pedunculate Water-starwort
Intermediate Water star-wort
Short-leaved Water-starwort

Those with more oval leaves
Various-leaved Water-starwort
Blunt-fruited Water-starwort

Because they grow in water, it is often impractical to get close to them.

THE PLANTAIN FAMILY PLANTAGINACEAE

Plants have a basal rosette of leaves with leafless stems growing out of them. The stems carry a flowering spike and the bright yellow stamens project outwards so that the spike looks like a small fireworks sparkler.

Buck's-horn Plantain Plantago coronopus (AP 161)

Rosette leaves much divided. Stems often start at an angle and then straighten. Usually in sandy/gravely soil. *Height - 10 cms*

THE PLANTAIN FAMILY Cont'd....

Sea Plantain

Plantago maritima (AP 161)

Leaves long, narrow and grass like.
Height - 15 cms

Low growing. Hairless.

Ribwort Plantain

Plantago lanceolata (AP 161)

Leaves long, narrow and with obvious
network of veins.
Height - 30 cms

Flower spike short, cone shaped and
green/brown with long stamen.

Hoary Plantain

Plantago media (AP 161)

Leaves are broad oval and downy. Flower spike long, oval with pink anthers.
Height - 30 cms

THE PLANTAIN FAMILY Cont'd....

Greater Plantain   Plantago major   (AP 161)

Leaves pointed, oval, large (10 cms long); veins obvious. Anthers purple.
Flower spike long and thin. *Height - 30 cms*

Shoreweed   Littorella uniflora   (AP 162)

A rare plant, usually submerged, or on mud in acidic water. Leaves are grass like but
semi-circular in section. They are short, about 10 cms, but the plant puts out long,
rooting runners. The flowers are small and greenish with the male flowers at the top of
the stem and the female flowers at the bottom.

THE BUDDLEJA FAMILY   BUDDLEJACEAE

Butterfly-bush   Buddleja davidii   (AP 162)

Medium sized bush. Leaves grey-green and opposite, long, narrow-oval.
Flowers blue-purple in long triangular heads.
Height - 4 metres

THE ASH FAMILY   OLEACEAE

Trees or shrubs. The group comprises Ash, Lilac and Privet as well as garden escapes such as Forsythia etc.

Ash   Fraxinus excelsior   (AP 162)

A large tree. Leaves pinnate with about 5 pairs of opposite leaflets. Twigs grey with black buds.

Flowers, without petals, in dark clusters. Seed cases are ash keys. *Height - 30 metres*

Lilac   Syringa vulgaris   (AP 163)

Shrub. Leaves heart-shaped. Purple or white flowers in tapering spikes. *Height - 5 metres*

THE ASH FAMILY Cont'd....

Wild Privet

Ligustrum vulgare (AP 163)

Shrub with longish narrow leaves. Clusters of scented white flowers.
Fruit is shiny black berry. *Height - 3 metres*

Garden Privet

Ligustrum ovalifolium (AP 163)

Shrub with round-oval
leaves. Fruit shiny-black
berries. Small spires of
white scented flowers.
Height - 3 metres

THE FIGWORT FAMILY

SCROPHULARIACEAE

The flowers have five petals, usually with lower petals protruding to form a lip. The Family
includes Mulleins, Toadflaxes, Figworts, Speedwells and some semi-parasitic species.

The Mullein group

Yellow or white flowers on tall spires. Usually downy or hairy.

White Mullein

Verbascum lychnitis (AP 164)

Height - 1.5 metres

Angled stem has
side branches
like a cande-
labrum. Stem
covered in sticky
down. Leaves
downy on the
underside.
Flowers white
(15 mms) across.

THE FIGWORT FAMILY Cont'd....

Hungarian Mullein   **Verbascum speciosum   (AP 164)**

A very rare introduction. General growth pattern is like White Mullein but in this case the flowers are yellow. *Height - 1.5 metres*

Moth Mullein   **Verbascum blattaria   (AP 163)**

Solitary
flowers on
short stalks.
Single spike.
Flowers
usually yellow
but sometimes
white.

Height - 1 metre

Great Mullein   **Verbascum thapsus (AP 164)**

Tall (2 metres) spire with only minor side branches near the base.
Flowers yellow (20 mms across). Face of flower is concave.
Stem round. Leaf stalks winged and clasping stem. *Height - 2 metres*

THE FIGWORT FAMILY Cont'd....

Dark Mullein

Flower stem largely unbranched. Leaves slightly hairy and with distinct leaf stalk. *Height - 1 metre*

Verbascum nigrum   (AP 164)

Petals yellow and often with purple markings at the base. Stamens covered in purple hairs.

The Figwort Group

Plants have square stems and opposite leaves. In the first two species, the flowers have an open 'mouth', the petals are a reddish brown.

Water Figwort

Square stem and distinct wings. Upper petals reddish-brown. Leaves often have a pair of small leaflets near the leaf stalk. Grows near water. *Height - 1 metre*

Scrophularia auriculata   (AP 165)

THE FIGWORT FAMILY Cont'd....

Common Figwort

Scrophularia nodosa   (AP 164)

Usually in woodland shade. Square stems without wings. Leaf stalks without leaflets.
Height - 80 cms

Cape Figwort

Phygelius capensis   (AP 165)

Flowers bright red with longish tube. Grows near water.
Petals less clearly divided into lips. *Height - 1 metre*

The Musk group

Large, bright yellow flowers with protruding lower lip. Grow in or near water.

Blood-drop-emlets

Mimulus luteus   (AP 166)

Bright yellow petals with pattern of red blotches. Sprawling growth. Leaves broad.
Height - 40 cms

THE FIGWORT FAMILY Cont'd....

Monkeyflower

Height - 60 cms

Mimulus guttatus (AP 165)

Plant is sprawling and hairless. Grows in, or near water. Large (30 mms) yellow flowers. Flowers have small red dots in throat.

Musk

Height - 30 cms

Mimulus moschatus (AP 165)

Small (15 mms) flowers without red spots. Plant hairy. More upright stems. Grows in, or near water.

The Toadflax Group

Flowers like the garden snapdragon but usually smaller.

Snapdragon

Antirrhinum majus (AP 166)

Well known garden plant, now established as an escape. Flowers large (4 cms). Petals usually pink/red with yellow throat but colour is variable. Leaves oval.
Height - 60 cms

THE FIGWORT FAMILY Cont'd….

Common Toadflax

Linaria vulgaris (AP 167)

Tall (60 cms) with obvious yellow flowers in spikes. Leaves long, thin and greyish-green. Flowers about 25 cms long with an orange 'mouth' and a stout spur.
Height - 60 cms

Purple Toadflax

Linaria purpurea (AP 167)

Tall (80 cms) thin
spikes of purple flowers.
Leaves long, thin and grey-green.
Flower has long curved spur.
Height - 80 cms

Pale Toadflax

Linaria repens (AP 167)

Similar to
purple toadflax.
Flowers very
pale pinkish
purple.
Flowers have
short spur.
Leaves long,
thin and
grey-green.

Height - 70 cms

THE FIGWORT FAMILY Cont'd....

Ivy-leaved Toadflax

Cymbalaria muralis (AP 166)

Sprawling, often on old walls. Flowers purple with two yellow patches.
Short spur. Long flower stalks; leaves ivy-shaped. *Height - 50 cms*

Small Toadflax

Chaenorhinum minus (AP 166)

Flowers sparsely spread on long stalks. Flowers small (6 mms) and pale purple.
Leaves long, narrow and pointed. *Height - 20 cms*

Annual Toadflax

Linaria maroccana (AP 168)

Flower colour variable
but usually purple.
Leaves long and thin.
Flowers large (20 mms)
and bright, with long spur.
Height - 40 cms

THE FIGWORT FAMILY Cont'd....

Weasel's-snout

Misopates orontium (AP 166)

Stem tall (40 cms) slender and branched. Leaves strap-shaped and hairy.
Also known as Lesser Snapdragon. Flowers 12 mms long; pinkish red.
Height - 40 cms

Sharp-leaved Fluellen

Kickxia elatine (AP 167)

Prostrate, branching stem. Leaves are broadly arrow-shaped.
Flowers solitary on long stalk. Flowers yellow with purple upper lip and straight spur.
Height - 40 cms

Round-leaved Fluellen

Kickxia spuria (AP 167)

Similar to Sharp-leaved but leaves oval, hairy and sticky. Spur is curved.
Flowers with deep purple upper lip. *Height - 40 cms*

THE FIGWORT FAMILY Cont'd....

Foxglove Group

Foxglove   Digitalis purpurea (AP 168)

Tall (2 metres) spires of
purple 'gloves'.
Over winter has rosette
of large, hairy and oval
grey-green leaves.
Height - 2 metres

Straw Foxglove   Digitalis lutea (AP 168)

Spires of
yellow-cream
'gloves'.
The glove are
often tipped
with purple.
Long thin leaves

Height - 1.5 metres

Fairy Foxglove   Erinus alpinus (AP 168)

Small (25 cms),
clump forming.
Flowers small
(12 mms)
pink-purple in
terminal spikes.
Petals showing
five lobes rather
than a 'glove'.

Height - 1.5 metres

THE FIGWORT FAMILY Cont'd....

Speedwells

Low growing plants with small blue flowers. Leaves opposite. Seed pods can sometimes help in identification.

Ivy-leaved Speedwell   Veronica hederifolia (AP 170)

Sprawling growth, stem branches near the base. Ivy-shaped grey-green downy leaves. A very common garden weed. Flowers small (5 mms) and lilac-blue with darker stripes. Petals slightly longer than the sepals. Seed pods with two sections very close together.
Height - sprawls to 20 cms

Common Field-speedwell   Veronica persica (AP 170)

Sprawling growth, reddish, hairy stems. Flowers clustered together on the stem. Upper petals (about 10 mms) blue with darker veins. Lower petal pale. Leaves, roughly rounded, pale-green and toothed. Seed pod consists of two diverging pale lobes.
Height - 40 cms

Green Field-speedwell   Veronica agrestis (AP 170)

Petals pale
blue except for
white lower
petal.
Leaves pale
green. Seed
pod heart-
shaped with
straight hairs.

Height - 20 cms

THE FIGWORT FAMILY Cont'd....

Grey Field-speedwell

Veronica polita   (AP 170)

Similar to Green Field-speedwell but flowers (6mms) dark blue. Sprawling growth. Leaves grey-green. Seed pod oblong with small notch and hooked hairs. Sepals pointed and largely covering the seed pods. *Height - 20 cms*

Slender Speedwell

Veronica filiformis   (AP 170)

Mat forming. Flowers (10 mms) purple-blue with a pale lip. Leaves bright green, kidney shaped and lobed. Leaves opposite on non-flowering stems, but alternate on flowering stems.

Height - sprawls to 30 cms

Germander Speedwell

Veronica chamaedrys   (AP 168)

Sprawling growth with opposite, oval, toothed leaves. Flowers large (10 mms) clear blue with white centre and close together on the stem. Stem has two lines of white hairs, one on each side. *Height - 30 cms*

THE FIGWORT FAMILY Cont'd....

Wood Speedwell

Veronica montana (AP 169)

Similar to Germander Speedwell but stems hairy all round. Petals have pink tinge.
Leaves have distinct stalks. *Height - 25 cms*

Wall Speedwell

Veronica arvensis (AP 170)

Often found on walls or in poor thin soil. Lower leaves with stalks, upper leaves close to
stem. Flowers very small (2 mms), bright blue and on short (7 cms) upright stems.
Height - 15 cms

Thyme-leaved Speedwell

Veronica serpyllifolia (AP 168)

Low creeping growth. Leaves narrow-oval and growing close to upright stem.
Petals pale blue almost white with dark stripes. *Height - 20 cms*

THE FIGWORT FAMILY Cont'd....

Heath Speedwell   Veronica officinalis (AP 168)

Low creeping
growth; mat
forming.
Leaves oval,
toothed and on
short stalks.
Petals lilac.

Height - 20 cms

Speedwells with upright stems and growing in or near water.

Pink Water-speedwell   Veronica catenata (AP 169)

Grows in water. Flowers pink (an exception in the Speedwells) in loose spikes.
Flowering branches and some leaves above water. Stem often reddish.
Leaves long, thin and slightly toothed. *Height above water 25 cms*

Blue Water-speedwell   Veronica anagallis-aquatica (AP 169)

Grows in water. Leaves long and thin and without teeth. Flowers blue, in tight spikes.
Flowering branches and some leaves above water. *Height above water surface - 25 cms*

THE FIGWORT FAMILY Cont'd....

Brooklime

Veronica beccabunga (AP 169)

Grows in ditches, streams etc. Leaves bright green, roundish and toothed.

Flowers bright blue in paired spikes.
Height – 40 cms

Marsh Speedwell

Veronica scutellata (AP 169)

Usually on wet, acid soil. Leaves, often brown, small, narrow and finely toothed. Few pale blue flowers on long stalks and in loose clusters.
Height – 15 cms

Other members of the Family

Apart from Cornish Moneywort, they are semi-parasites. They use their leaves (often quite small) to make some food for themselves but they also attach themselves through their root system to other plants and "steal" nutrients from them. The grasses in a meadow infested with Yellow Rattle are noticeably smaller.

Cornish Moneywort

Sibthorpia europaea (AP 171)

A small delicate mat-growing plant. Quite rare, normally growing in boggy ground especially on Exmoor. Leaves round and lobed.
Flowers solitary, very small (2 mms) and without lips. Two white and three pink petals.
Height - 15 cms

THE FIGWORT FAMILY Cont'd....

Common Cow-wheat

Melampyrum pratense (AP 171)

Flowers pale yellow in opposite pairs, but usually turned so that both face same way. Leaves long and narrow. Stem inclined to sprawl. Petals form long tube (15 mms) ending in small upper lip and bulbous lower one. *Height - 25 cms*

Red Bartsia

Odontites vernus (AP 173)

Flowering spikes of dull purple-red flowers. Leaves long (20 mms) and narrow. Leaves and stem often have purplish tinge. Flowers small (8 mms) with tube and paler lips.

Height - 25 cms

Yellow Bartsia

Parentucellia viscosa (AP 173)

Short (25 cms) sturdy, hairy stem. Flowers in loose spikes. Petals yellow with hood and lower lip. Lip has three lobes. *Height - 25 cms*

262

THE FIGWORT FAMILY Cont'd....

Yellow-rattle

Rhinanthus minor (AP 173)

Semi-parasite on grasses.
Petals yellow with large hood.
Sepals form bladder which
holds seeds - (rattles).
Leaves long and toothed.
Height - 30 cms

Lousewort

Pedicularis sylvatica (AP 173)

Short (15 cms), fleshy and clump
forming. Petals pale pink with hood and
three lobed darker lips.

Leaves pinnate, leaflets toothed.
Height - 15 cms

Marsh Lousewort

Pedicularis palustris (AP 173)

Similar to common Lousewort but taller
(50 cms); grows more upright.
Height - 50 cms

Petal tube pale but open end of the
flower is a deeper pink/purple.

THE FIGWORT FAMILY Cont'd….

The Eyebright members of the Family

An extremely difficult group to separate out, the difference between the species are very slight and the species hybridise freely. It is easier to treat them as a group under the title Eyebright aggregates.

Eyebright   Euphrasia agg. (AP 171)

Low growing (20 cms) and often mat forming. Leaves oval/round and clearly toothed. Petals white and cream with purple markings. Petals form an upper hood and forked lower lip.
Height - 20 cms

THE BROOMRAPE FAMILY   OROBANCHACEAE

Parasitic plants without green leaves.

Toothwort   Lathraea squamaria (AP 174)

Usually parasitic on Hazel. Stem white or very pale pink. Flowers pinkish white. Flowers have two lips and are in one-sided spikes.

Height - 25 cms

Ivy Broomrape   Orobanche hederae (AP 174)

Grows on ivy. Petals creamy-white with purple veins. Lower lip with three lobes.
Height - 30 cms

THE BROOMRAPE FAMILY Cont'd...

Greater Broomrape   Orobanche rapum-genistae (AP 174)

Very rare and subject to seasonal fluctuations. Usually on Broom or Gorse.
Upper lip hooded, lower lip with three lobes. Bulbous base to stem. Flowers large (20 mms); petals yellow with purple tinge. *Height - 50 cms*

Common Broomrape   Orobanche minor (AP 174)

Height - 50 cms

Common in meadows. Stem brownish. Petals with off-white tips changing to purple tubes. Upper lip with two lobes, lower lip with three. Back of the petal tube is arched.

THE BUTTERWORT/BLADDERWORT FAMILY   LENTIBULARIACEAE

The Butterworts live in marshy habitats: the Bladderworts live in water. Both groups use their leaves in the normal way but they also use them to trap small invertebrates.

Large-flowered Butterwort   Pinguicula grandiflora (AP 175)

Five large purple petals arranged in a trumpet shape and with a long spur at the back. The lower lip petal has a notch. Stem emerges from a rosette of pale green, oval leaves.

The leaves are sticky to trap insects. Rosette does not persist over winter. *Height - 20 cms*

THE BUTTERWORT/BLADDERWORT FAMILY Cont'd...

Pale Butterwort   Pinguicula lusitanica (AP 175)

Height - 10 cms

Basal rosette of small in-rolled pale-green leaves. Leaf rosettes persist during winter. Flowers small, very pale lilac on a stem about 10 cms long. Flowers has long spur.

Greater Bladderwort   Utricularia vulgaris (AP 175)

Yellow flowers appear on stems about 10 cms above the water surface. Petals form a hood, a lip and a central mouth. Lower lip petal folds back along its length.
The leaves, totally aquatic, are finely divided and studded with trapping bladders.
Plant rootless. *Height above water - 10 cms*

Bladderwort   Utricularia australis (AP 175)

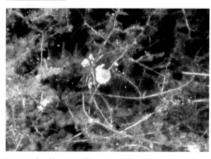

Very similar to Greater Bladderwort. Lower lips has wavy edge and does not fold back.
Height above water - 10 cms

THE BUTTERWORT/BLADDERWORT FAMILY Cont'd...

Lesser Bladderwort

Utricularia minor (AP 175)

Flowers small (5 mms) and very pale
yellow. Stem about 6 cms above water.
Height above water - 6 cms

Flowers small (5 mms) and
very pale yellow.

THE BELLFLOWER FAMILY

CAMPANULACEAE

Flowers are bell-shaped and, apart from Cornish Bellflower are blue. In size the plants
range from very low-growing mat forming clumps to one metre tall spires.

Cornish Bellflower

Campanula alliariifolia   (AP 176)

Spires of drooping white bells. Clump forming.
Leaves triangular/heart-shaped and toothed. *Height - 40 cms*

Sheep's-bit

Jasione montana (AP 177)

Mass of small blue flowers packed into a
scabious-like' head. Petals powder blue.

Leaves narrow, oblong and downy.
Height - 25 cms

267

THE BELLFLOWER Cont'd…

Clustered Bellflower

Height - 60 cms

Campanula glomerata (AP 176)

Flowers in a compact head but easily distinguished from each other. Petals a deep purple-blue. Lower leaves oval and toothed, upper leaves clasp stem.

Peach-leaved Bellflower

Campanula persicifolia (AP 176)

Height - 60 cms

Flowers large, cup-shaped and blue (very occasionally white). Flowers on slender upright stems. Leaves long and narrow. Usually a garden escape.

Ivy-leaved Bellflower

Wahlenbergia hederacea (AP 177)

Low growing (10 cms) in boggy, acidic soil. Creeping stem.
Flowers pale-blue, usually one on each stalk. Leaves with pointed lobes.
Height - 10 cms

THE BELLFLOWER Cont'd...

Adria Bellflower Campanula portenschlagiana (AP 176)

Low, spreading, mat forming. Flowers blue and bell-shaped but with five distinct outer lobes. Leaves pointed and toothed. *Height - 15 cms*

Trailing Bellflower Campanula poscharskyana (AP 176)

Low growing with central clump and long prostrate stems spreading outwards. Flowers blue. Flowers start as bells but then open out and become star-like.
Leaves pointed, oval and toothed. *Height - 20 cms*

Harebell Campanula rotundifolia (AP 177)

Slender stem with a few narrow leaves. In the north of Britain this is sometimes known as 'Bluebell'. Flowers, few to a stem, are pale blue bells. *Height - 25 cms*

269

Venus's-looking-glass   **Legousia hybrida (AP 177)**

Flowers with short bell-like tube opening
into flat-faced five-lobed stars.
Petals purple. Leaves narrow oval.
This photo is of the larger
cultivated variety.
Height - 20 cms

The remaining four members of this Family are relatively tall (70 cms to 1 metre).
They have bell-shaped flowers on upright stems.

Nettle-leaved Bellflower   **Campanula trachelium (AP 176)**

Leaves triangular and strongly toothed.
Small number of flowers in spikes at top
of stem.

Height - 80 cms

THE BELLFLOWER Cont'd...

Chimney Bellflower   Campanula pyramidalis (AP 176)

Growth form somewhat like a foxglove. Tall stems in clumps with flower-heads all facing the same way. Leaves oval, pointed and slightly toothed. *Height - 1 metre*

Creeping Bellflower   Campanula rapunculoides (AP 177)

Flowers on upright stems. Flowers often have purplish tinge; individual flowers hang downwards on the stem. It gets its name from the creeping rootstock. *Height - 70cms*

Giant Bellflower   Campanula latifolia (AP 176)

 Pale blue flowers on long spikes; sepals very narrow. Stem is bluntly angled. Leaves narrow-oval and slightly toothed.

Height – 1 metre

THE BEDSTRAW FAMILY   RUBIACEAE

Most are weak scrambling
climbers. The leaves are arranged
round the stem in whorls.
The stem is usually four-sided.
Leaves have spines or hooks.
The flowers are small and
usually have 4 petals.

Lady's Bedstraw   ### Galium verum   (AP 179)

Creeping stem with erect flowering shoots. Leaves small with edges in-rolled.
Smells of hay. Bright yellow flowers in dense clusters.
Height - 60 cms

Crosswort   ### Cruciata laevipes   (AP 180)

Softly hairy stems. Leaves in whorls of four, each leaf with three veins.
Flowers pale yellow. Fruits are black berries.
Height - 40 cms

Three species have pink flowers.

Caucasian Crosswort   **Phuopsis stylosa (AP 178)**

A garden escape. Sprawling stems leading to mat formation. Terminal clusters
(3 cms across) of five petalled pink flowers. Leaves in close whorls of eight.
Height of mat - 20 cms

Squinancywort   **Asperula cynanchica (AP 178)**

Low growing with square prickly stems. Leaves in whorls of six. Stiff leaves form ruff
immediately below head. Very pale pink flowers in small compact heads.
Height - 20 cms

Field Madder   **Sherardia arvensis (AP 178)**

Low growing. Square, prickly stem. Leaves in whorls of six. Pink flowers in small
compact heads with a ruff of leaves below the head. *Horizontal spread - 20 cms*

Not pink flowers.

Wild Madder   **Rubia peregrina (AP 180)**

Scrambling climber. Flower with five yellow-green petals. Stem square.
Leaves edged with small prickles, in whorls of five. Fruit is clusters of black berries.
Height - 1.5 metres

Bedstraws with white flowers

Slender Bedstraw   **Galium pumilum (AP 179)**

Slender plant with square stem. Flowers creamy-white, small (2mms). Leaves in whorls
of about eight, leaves have prickly edges and a bristle at the tip. *Height - 25 cms*

Cleavers (Goosegrass)   **Galium aparine (AP 180)**

Often forms 'curtains' in hedgerows. Flowers small (2mms),
whitish green. Plant covered in backwards pointing prickles.
Leaves in whorls of about seven, stem square.
Seed pods hard, in pairs, and covered in hooks.
Height 2 metres

THE BEDSTRAW FAMILY Cont'd...

Woodruff

Galium odoratum (AP 178)

Scented, usually ground cover in woodland. Leaves in whorls of about seven, whorls look like rosettes. Flowers white. *Height - 30 cms*

Fen Bedstraw

Galium uliginosum (AP 178)

Weak sprawling growth, usually in water. Stem has backward pointing prickles. Leaves in whorls of 6 to 8. Flowers white and small. Leaves have a small bristle at the top; this is often easier to feel than to see. *Height - 40 cms*

Common Marsh-Bedstraw

Galium palustre (AP 179)

Weak sprawling growth, usually in water. Stem rough but without prickles. Leaves in whorls of 4 or 5 and without bristles at tip. Flowers white and small. *Height - 60 cms*

275

THE BEDSTRAW FAMILY Cont'd...

Heath Bedstraw

Galium saxatile (AP 180)

Usually on acidic soils. Sprawling and often mat forming. Leaves in whorls of about 6. leaves edged with fine forward pointing prickles. Flowers creamy white and small.
Height - 20 cms

Hedge Bedstraw

Galium mollugo (AP 179)

Scrambling, climbing to
about 1 metre.
Leaves oval and in whorls of
about 10.
Flowers white, petals
pointed at tip.
Height - 1 metre

HONEYSUCKLE FAMILY

CAPRIFOLIACEAE

Shrubs or woody plants, often climbers. Leaves opposite in pairs. Flowers vary but based on pattern of five petals fused at the base into a tube and opening with lips. Five sepals. The first member of this Family is not in the popular image of a Honeysuckle. It is usually grown as a hedging plant in the garden.

Wilson's Honeysuckle

Lonicera nitida (AP 182)

Leaves small (10 mms) and
dark green. Very small
yellow-cream flowers.
Fruits are purple berries.
Height – 2 metres

HONEYSUCKLE FAMILY Cont'd...

Perfoliate Honeysuckle

Leaves fused so that stem appears to grow through them.
Height - 5 metres

Lonicera caprifolium (AP 183)

Flowers tubular, bright orange-red. Fruits are red berries.

Japanese Honeysuckle

Woody evergreen climber. Flowers white/yellow with distinct lemony scent.

Lonicera japonica   (AP 183)

Fruits are black berries.
Height - 6 metres

Honeysuckle

Lonicera periclymenum (AP 183)

Leaves grey-green. Flowers creamy-yellow in pairs. Flower stalk downy. Fruits are red berries.
Height - 3 metres

Himalayan Honeysuckle

Shrub with sappy upright stems. Stems often live only one year. Leaves pointed.
Height - 1.5 metres

Leycesteria formosa (AP 182)

Flowers red, purple and white in downwards hanging tassles.
Fruits are purple berries.

Snowberry

Symphoricarpos albus (AP 182)

Shrub with slender upright stems.
Clump forming.
Flowers small and mainly pink.
Fruits are white berries which persist after leaf fall.
Height - 2 metres

HONEYSUCKLE FAMILY Cont'd...

But not with typical "Honeysuckle" type flowers. This group has numerous white flowers in a flattish white head.

Elder   **Sambucus nigra (AP 180)**

Small tree with grey-brown furrowed bark. Creamy white flowers in flat topped sprays. Leaves pinnate. Fruits are black-purple berries.
Height - 10 metres

Dwarf Elder   **Sambucus ebulus (AP 181)**

Non-woody vertical stems. Stems die back in Winter. Leaves light-green and pinnate. Flowers white with pink tipped petals. Flowers cluster to form a domed head.

Height - 2 metres

Guelder-rose   **Viburnum opulus (AP 181)**

A woodland under-shrub with ivy-shaped leaves; each leaf with 3 to 5 toothed lobes.. White flowers in large heads. Outer flowers have larger petals than the inner ones. Fruits are red berries. *Height - 2.5 metres*

279

HONEYSUCKLE FAMILY Cont'd...

Wayfaring-tree   **Viburnum lantana (AP 181)**

Usually a hedgerow shrub. Leaves oval and silvery-downy on underside.
White flowers in flat topped clusters, prominent red-brown stamens.
Fruits are berries which become red and then turn black. *Height - 4 metres*

THE MOSCHATEL FAMILY   ADOXACEAE

There is only one member of this Family recorded in the *Atlas*.

Moschatel   **Adoxa moschatellina (AP 183)**

Very small (10 cms) plant,
usually in woodland.
Flower heads with pale
green petals. Head has four
faces (Town-Hall Clock)
and one facing upwards.
Basal leaves with 3 lobes.
Height - 10 cms

THE VALERIAN FAMILY   VALERIANACEAE

Herbaceous plants. Leaves opposite and without stipules. Petals funnel-shaped; flowers
in compact heads.

Cornsalad group

Flowers very small and pale bluish/lilac colour. Five petals. Flowers grouped into heads.

Common Cornsalad   **Valerianella locusta (AP 183)**

Hairless; lower leaves spoon-shaped, upper leaves slightly toothed. Flowers in tightly
packed heads. Petals pale pink –purple. Sepals very small. Seed case is hazel-nut shaped,
but very small. *Height - 30 cms*

HONEYSUCKLE FAMILY Cont'd...

Keeled-fruited Cornsalad   Valerianella carinata (AP 183)

Leaves broad and bluntly toothed. Sepals very small. Flowers lilac in tight head.
Seed case egg-shaped with prominent ridge. *Height - 30 cms*

Narrow-fruited Cornsalad   Valerianella dentata (AP 183)

Flower head less compact. Seed case flask shaped. Leaves long and narrow with a small
projecting lobe at the base.

The Valerian Group

Flowers in compact heads. Petals usually pink, funnel-shaped.

Red Valerian   Centranthus ruber (AP 184)

Leaves grey-green. Usually on rock or wall surfaces. Flowers red, pink or white
in clusters. Five petals, tubular with short spur. One stamen protrudes.
Height - 75 cms

281

Common Valerian

Valeriana officinalis (AP 184)

Tall (1.5 metres). Flower made up of five pink petals.
Individual flowers combined into large head.
Leaves pinnate with about 5 pairs of leaflets.
Height - 1.5 metres

Marsh Valerian

Valeriana dioica (AP 184)

Smaller (25 cms) each with pale pink petals in a tight head. Occurs in marshy ground.
Leaves pinnate, usually four pairs of leaflets. *Height - 25 cms*

THE TEASEL FAMILY   DIPSACACEAE

Teasels and Scabious species. Upright stems. Large compact flower heads with ring
of bracts.

Wild Teasel

Dipsacus fullonum (AP 184)

Despite the scientific name, this is not the Fullers Teasel. Strongly erect prickly stems.
Flower heads egg-shaped with purple flowers ripening in belts.
Flower head has straight spines. Leaves opposite and fused at the base to form a cup.
Height - 2 metres

THE TEASEL FAMILY Cont'd...

Fuller's Teasel   Dipsacus sativus (AP 185)

Similar to Wild Teasel but the spines are hooked; was used in "fulling" cloth. *Height - 2 metres*

Small Teasel   Dipsacus pilosus (AP 185)

Branched stem with few prickles. Stem leaves long, narrow and not fused across the stem. Flower heads small and round. Petals pale pink. *Height - 2 metres*

Giant Scabious   Cephalaria gigantea (AP 185)

Tall (2 metres). Yellow flower heads.
Leaves pinnate.
Height - 2 metres

THE TEASEL FAMILY Cont'd…

Field Scabious   Knautia arvensis (AP 185)

Hairy stem. Lower stem leaves pinnate. Pale blue flowers in round heads (3cms across).
Each flower has 5 lobes. Marginal flowers larger than the central ones.
Height - 70 cms

Small Scabious   Scabiosa columbaria (AP 185)

Branching stem. Stem leaves pinnate. A smaller version of Field Scabious.
Pale blue flowers in round heads (2 to 3 cms across), each flower has 4 lobes.
Marginal flowers bigger than the central ones. *Height - 50 cms*

Devil's-bit Scabious   Succisa pratensis (AP 185)

Leaves long, narrow
and toothed.
Flowers bluish purple.
Individual flowers all
same size. Round heads
about 2 cms across.
Individual flowers as well
as heads have long spiky
bracts. Leaves long
narrow and toothed.

Height - 40 cms

THE DAISY FAMILY   ASTERACEAE (COMPOSITAE)

The Family gets its alternative name, Compositae, because the flower heads are made up of a collection of flowers (florets) standing on a single head. The head is called the capitulum.

The flowers may have strap-shaped petals or tubular ones or, in a few cases the petals are so small or even absent that they give little or no colour to the flower.

The head is usually surrounded by bracts which look like sepals.

Although it cuts across the normal botanical classification, for the non-expert it is easier to divide the Family on the basis of petal colour.

The Family can then be divided into the following groups: -

Those with blue flowers.
The thistles with purplish heads, no distinct centre and prickly stems.
Those not thistles but with purplish or pinkish flowers.
Those with insignificant petals, the flowers appearing green or brown.
The daisy group, i.e. those with white outer petals and a centre of yellow ones.
The dandelion group, i.e. those with all yellow flowers.

The Blue flower group (the smallest one).

Chicory   Cichorium intybus (AP 189)

Bright-blue flowers on a branching stem. Leaves narrow, lower ones toothed. Flowers about 3 cms across.
Height - 80 cms

Cornflower   Centaurea cyanus (AP 189)

Flowers with blue petals; flower head about 2 cms across. The flowers are on an oval head. The outer flowers are large, tube-shaped, opening like a hand.

Height - 50 cms

THE DAISY FAMILY Cont'd...

Perennial Cornflower   **Centaurea montana (AP 189)**

Flower with blue petals; flower head about 5 cms across. The flowers are on an almost round base covered in green bracts. Leaves oval and downy. The outer flowers are large, tube-shaped opening like the fingers of a hand. *Height - 60 cms*

Blue Globe-thistle   **Echinops bannaticus (AP 186)**

Round head of blue flowers. Sharply toothed leaves. Leaves downy grey on underside. *Height - 2 metres*

Common Blue-sow-thistle   **Cicerbita macrophylla (AP 192)**

Head of several lilac-blue flowers. Leaves toothed with large terminal lobe. Soft prickly stem. *Height - 50 cms*

THE DAISY FAMILY Cont'd…

Blue Fleabane   Erigeron acer (AP 200)

Flowers in a number of loose heads. Outer petals blue-purple. Leaves long and narrow.
Height - 50 cms

The Thistle Group

Apart from Carline Thistle, they have purple flower heads. Stems and leaves spiny.
Whole plant 'thistly'. Seed heads like "Dandelion clocks".

Carline Thistle   Carlina vulgaris (AP 186)

The only one with a
yellow flower head.
Flower soon fades leaving
a straw-coloured ring of
bracts. Upper leaves
clasp stem.
Height - 40 cms

Dwarf Thistle   Cirsium acaule (AP 187)

Purple flower head sits more or less
stemless in basal rosette of spiny leaves.
Height - 15 cms

THE DAISY FAMILY Cont'd…

Milk Thistle   Silybum marianum (AP 188)

Flowers large (40 cms) born singly. Leaves with milky-white veins. *Height - 1 metre*

Meadow Thistle   Cirsium dissectum (AP 187)

Stems short (25 cms), each stem carrying one purple flower head. Stems not very prickly. Leaves long and narrow, toothed rather than deeply divided. *Height - 25 cms*

Musk Thistle   Carduus nutans (AP 187)

Large (40 cms) drooping heads. Flower heads purple with a frill of turned-back bracts. *Height - 1 metre*

288

THE DAISY FAMILY Cont'd...

Spear Thistle   Cirsium vulgare (AP 187)

Leaves pinnate
and very spiny.
Leaves end in
a long pointed
tip. Flowers
purple and
about 30 mms
across.

Height - 1 metre

Woolly Thistle   Cirsium eriophorum (AP 187)

Large rounded head with a tuft of purple florets.
The pinnate leaves have an extra row which project upwards from the mid-rib of the leaf.
Height - 1.5 metres

Marsh Thistle   Cirsium palustre (AP 188)

Tall (1.5
metres), upright
and usually with
a purple tinge.
Stem very
spiney. Flower
heads small
(15 mms),
purple and
usually in
clusters.

Height - 1.5 metres

THE DAISY FAMILY Cont'd...

Cotton Thistle   Onopordum acanthium (AP 188)

Very tall (2 metres). Stem with wings and toothed leaves. Both covered in white cottony down. Flowers (40 mms across) pale purple heads with spiny bracts.
Height - 2 metres

Creeping Thistle   Cirsium arvense (AP 188)

Very common, usually forming clumps. Creeping rootstock.
Flowers small (20 mms long) and 10 mms wide; lilac colour.
Leaves with spiny lobes.
Height - 1.5 metres

Slender Thistle   Carduus tenuiflorus (AP 186)

Mostly restricted to the sandy coasted regions.
Very spiny stem, with broad spiny wings.
Flowers reddish purple.
Flower heads on long stalks, the stalks in clusters.
Height - 60 cms

THE DAISY FAMILY Cont'd...

Welted Thistle   Carduus crispus (AP 187)

Continuous spiny wing spiralling
all the way up the stem, except
for short distance under the
flower. Flower heads purple
and in small clusters.
Height - 1.0 metres

Pink or purple flowers (but not thistles) group.
Those with a yellow centre.

Sea Aster   Aster tripolium (AP 200)

Some flowers are daisy-like with a yellow centre and lilac outer petals. Other flower
heads have no or few outer strap petals. Stems tall (1 metre) and upright. Leaves long,
narrow and fleshy; have prominent mid-rib. Usually near the coast. *Height - 1 metre*

Mexican Fleabane   Erigeron karvinskianus (AP 200)

Sprawling, with pink or white daisy-like flowers. Flowers in loose clusters.
Leaves narrow, oval and in whorls. *Height - 50 cms*

291

THE DAISY FAMILY Cont'd...

Michaelmas-daisy

Aster species (AP 199)

This includes several garden escapes and hybrids. Distinguishing between them is best left to the experts. All have a central mass of yellow flowers surrounded by outer strap flowers in shades from purple-blue to lilac.

Stems erect and clump forming.
Height - 1.5 metres

Seaside Daisy

Erigeron glaucus (AP 200)

Clump forming with rosettes of round fleshy leaves. Sprawling growth.
Flowers with blue-purple outer ring and inner yellow centre. *Height - 30 cms*

Pink/purple flowers without a yellow centre but not Thistles.

Salsify

Tragopogon porrifolius (AP 191)

Dull-purple flower heads of strap-shaped petals. Green bracts, longer than the petals.
Upright stems and long thin leaves. *Height - 80 cms*

292

THE DAISY FAMILY Cont'd...

Hemp-agrimony

Eupatorium cannabinum (AP 209)

Individually small pink flowers but in dense trusses. Leaves palmate with toothed leaflets. Flowers soon fade to a dull straw colour.

Height - 1.25 metres

Butterbur

Petasites hybridus (AP 207)

Clump forming; only male flowers recorded; flowers in late Spring. Stem has large leaf-like bracts. Leaves large (80 mms), heart-shaped and toothed. Not scented.
Height - 60 cms

The "giant" form. The leaves are small but the plant can grow to 1 metre.

There is some similarity between Butterburs and Winter Heliotrope. The Heliotrope flowers in the Winter, is strongly scented, has loose flower heads and is smaller.

Winter Heliotrope

Petasites fragrans (AP 207)

Upright stem with clusters of lilac flowers. Leaves kidney-shaped and either not toothed or very finely toothed. Flowers in Winter. Scented.

Height-30 cms

THE DAISY FAMILY Cont'd...

Common Knapweed   Centaurea nigra (AP 189)

In the usual form, the flowers open to show branched outer rays, but in some forms the outer ray petals are absent. Flowers are bright purple. Stems are upright, leaves narrow; both hairy. *Height - 60 cms*

Greater Knapweed   Centaurea scabiosa (AP 188)

Purple flowers at the top of the head, the outer ones strap-shaped and divided. Leaves pinnate.

Tall (1 metre) wiry stems. Head of green and black bracts. *Height - 1 metre*

Saw-wort   Serratula tinctoria (AP 188)

Flowers made up of clusters of purple petals and heads of greenish, brown bracts. The petals (florets) do not show a clear distinction between the inner tubular ones and the outer strap shaped ones. The lowers leaves are pinnate, the upper ones long and narrow. *Height - 70 cms*

THE DAISY FAMILY Cont'd...

Greater Burdock   Arctium lappa (AP 186)

Tall (2 metres) bushy plant. Large head (30 mms across) with hooked bristles.
Solid leaf stalks and stems. Purple flowers in tight cluster at top of the head.
Leaves heart-shaped, toothed and as wide as long. *Height - 2 metres*

Lesser Burdock   Arctium minus (AP 186)

Less tall
(1.5 metres).
Flowers heads
20 mms across.
Purple flowers
in tight cluster
at top of head.
Leaves heart-
shaped, longer
than wide. Leaf
stalks hollow.

Height - 1.5 metres

Plants with very small flowers.
Only those of Pearly Everlasting have clearly coloured (white) petals.

Pearly Everlasting   Anaphalis margaritacea (AP 197)

Plant is downy white. Flowers small and with outer petals white and inner ones creamy.
Leaves downy, long and thin. *Height - 30 cms*

THE DAISY FAMILY Cont'd...

Common Cudweed

Filago vulgaris (AP 197)

White downy stems and leaves. Stems branch two or three times to make small clump. Flower heads in dense clusters; florets yellow. Leaves clasp the stem.
Height - 30 cms

Marsh Cudweed

Gnaphalium uliginosum (AP 197)

More bushy looking, lateral branches spreading. Flower heads in tight clusters, have brown look. Leaves long, narrow and downy but not stem clasping. Upper leaves form a ruff below the flower head.
Height - 20 cms

Mugwort

Height - 1 metres

Artemisia vulgaris (AP 201)

Tall (1 metre). Browny-grey flowers held erect. Bracts silvery. Leaves pinnate, leaflets toothed. Leaves green above and silvery-downy below. Stem and leaf veins often reddish.

THE DAISY FAMILY Cont'd...

Wormwood

Tall (1 metre). Silvery-grey flower heads which hang down and form loose clusters. Upper leaves long and narrow, lower leaves much divided.

Artemisia absinthium (AP 202)

Height - 1 metre

Sea Wormwood

Erect bushy stems covered in grey down. Grows on estuarine mud.
Height - 50 cms

Seriphidium maritimum (AP 201)

Flower heads small, yellow and packed together.

297

THE DAISY FAMILY Cont'd...

Pineappleweed

Short (30 cms) bushy plant; finely divided leaves. Whole plant smells of pineapple.

Matricaria discoidea (AP 204)

Flower heads like miniature pineapples.
Height - 30 cms

Daisy type group

Daisy-like flowers i.e. with a yellow centre and outer white ray petals.

Daisy

Well-known flower. Leaves spoon-shaped, fleshy, toothed and in a rosette.

Bellis perennis (AP 201)

Flower stalks leafless. Short (10 cms).
Height - 10 cms

THE DAISY FAMILY Cont'd…

Ox-eye Daisy   Leucanthemum vulgare (AP 203)

Tall (60 cms). Lower leaves spoon-shaped and toothed. Stem leaves clasp the stem, more clearly toothed or lobed. Flower heads daisy-like, large (4 cms across); typical Daisy form.
Height - 60 cms

Yarrow   Achillea millefolium (AP 202)

Tall (70 cms). Many small daisy-type heads packed closely together. Thus, plant appears to have several large, flat heads. Leaves much divided. Sometimes flowers have a pink tinge.
Height - 70 cms

Feverfew   Tanacetum parthenium (AP 201)

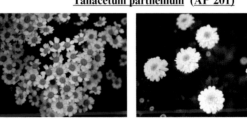

Much branched with pale lime-green leaves. Leaves pinnate; the leaflets lobed. Single flowers about 15 mms across but larger double forms often occur and the yellow centre is almost hidden.
Height - 50 cms

THE DAISY FAMILY Cont'd…

Sneezewort   Achillea ptarmica (AP 202)

Grey-green plant. Daisy like flowers in loose clusters.
Leaves long, narrow and finely toothed. *Height - 50 cms*

Mayweeds and Chamomiles

As their scientific names show, these very similar looking plants are members of four
different groups. Unfortunately, distinguishing between them often requires dismembering
a flower. The Chamomiles have scales between the yellow florets and the head which
carries the flowers is solid. They have domed flower heads which become conical with age.
The Mayweeds do not have the scales and the head of Scented Mayweed is hollow. The
centre of their flower heads start off as a flattish disc but becomes domed with age.

Chamomile   Chamaemelum nobile (AP 202)

Strongly scented and creeping. Underlying bracts have white edges. Leaves much
divided. White outer florets turn back to emphasise large, domed centre.
The head which carries the flower is solid. *Height - 30 cms but sprawls longer.*

Corn Chamomile   Anthemis arvensis (AP 203)

Faintly scented. Leaves divided but not very finely, have a fleshy look.
Underlying bracts tipped red/brown. *Height - 50 cms*

THE DAISY FAMILY Cont'd...

Stinking Chamomile   Anthemis cotula (AP 203)

Has unpleasant smell. Flower heads small (2 cms across). Leaves much divided.
Bracts have white edge and dark green mid rib. *Height - 40 cms*

Mayweeds

Daisy-like flowers with leaves divided many times. As the flowers mature, the central
domed head becomes flatter.

Scented Mayweed   Matricaria recutita (AP 203)

Strongly scented.
Leaves divided.
Outer white florets
soon bend back.

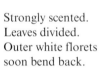

The flower head is hollow.
Underlying bracts
have a white border.
Height - 60 cms

Scentless Mayweed   Tripleurospermum inodorum (AP 204)

Not scented.
Bracts have a
brown border.
Leaves much divided.
Height - 70 cms

THE DAISY FAMILY Cont'd…

Sea Mayweed   **Tripleurospermum maritimum (AP 204)**

More bushy growth. Leaves divided but fleshier. Bracts have reddish-brown tips.
Height - 50 cms

Flower-heads with a compact yellow centre within a ring of flat yellow ray petals.

Colt's-foot   **Tussilago farfara (AP 206)**

Flowers early in the year (February).   One flower-head per stem.
Flower-heads emerge before the leaves.   Leaves heart–shape.
Stem short (15 cms) with scales.   *Height - 15 cms*

Sunflower   **Helianthus annuus (AP 207)**

 Tall (3 metres or
more) with one
large flower
head. Leaves
alternate, broad
oval and
pointed.
Centre of
flower-head
usually brown,
outer ray petals   *Height - 3 metres*
yellow.

302

THE DAISY FAMILY Cont'd…

Elecampane

Inula helenium (AP 198)

Tall (2.5 metres).
One flower-head on each stem.
Stems hairy.
Outer petals very narrow.
Leaves narrow-oval and toothed.
Height - 2.5 metres

Common Fleabane

Height - 80 cms

Pulicaria dysenterica (AP 198)

Usually near water. Leaves long and narrow, greyish-green and slightly fleshy. Leaf bases clasp the stem. Flower-heads (20 mms across) in flat topped clusters.

Leopard's-bane

Leaves alternate and downy on underside, toothed. Leaf bases clasp the stem.

Doronicum pardalianches (AP 206)

Large (60 mms) flower-head.
Height - 80 cms

THE DAISY FAMILY Cont'd…

Yellow Chamomile

Anthemis tinctoria (AP 203)

Flower-heads about 30 mms across, one per stem. Central compact head is domed.
Leaves pinnate. The only 'all-yellow' flower head with finely divided leaves.
Height - 50 cms

Corn Marigold

Chrysanthemum segetum (AP 203)

Flower-heads about 40 mms across, one per stem. Central disc is flat-topped.
Leaves long and lobed. Outer petals broad and soon fall back. *Height - 50 cms*

Ragworts

Have their flower-heads in clusters, most have bracts with dark tips.

Silver Ragwort

Senecio cineraria (AP 204)

Whole plant covered in silvery down. Short (50 cms). Flower-head forms a dome-shaped
cluster. Leaves pinnate with rounded leaflets. *Height - 50 cms*

THE DAISY FAMILY Cont'd...

Hoary Ragwort   **Senecio erucifolius (AP 205)**

Under-side of the leaves silvery-downy. Tall (1.5 metres). Flower-heads pale yellow.
Bracts without dark tips. Leaves pinnate with narrow leaflets.
Height - 1.5 metres

Broad-leaved Ragwort   **Senecio fluviatilis (AP 205)**

Numerous flower-heads but heads
have few (about 6) ray petals.
Lower leaves hairless, oval and toothed.
Upper leaves narrower.
Height - 1.5 metres

Marsh Ragwort   **Senecio aquaticus (AP 205)**

Plant well branched with flower-heads
at different heights. Ray petals well
separated. Stem often brown. Leaves
pinnate with large toothed end lobes.
Usually in marshy habitats.
Height - 60 cms

THE DAISY FAMILY Cont'd…

Oxford Ragwort   Senecio squalidus (AP 205)

Branched bushy plant with flower-heads just less than 20 mms across.
Inner row of black tipped bracts, outer row of much shorter ones.
Leaves smooth and glossy; pinnate or deeply lobed. *Height - 50 cms*

Common Ragwort   Senecio jacobaea (AP 205)

Very common. Flower-heads
in flat topped clusters. Bracts
dark tipped and almost all
of the same length. Leaves
deeply lobed or pinnate.

Height - 1.5 metres

Flowers yellow, small and compact, either button or shuttle-cock shaped.

Goldenrod   Solidago virgaurea (AP 198)

Flower-heads
small (8 mms)
in loose
spires.
Yellow ray
petals short.
Leaves long
and narrow.

Height - 60 cms

THE DAISY FAMILY Cont'd…

Canadian Goldenrod

Solidago canadensis (AP 199)

Tall (2 metres). Sprays of very small flower-heads on side branches.
Leaves long and toothed; young stem downy. The garden varieties are closely related.
Height - 2 metres

Early Goldenrod

Solidago gigantea (AP 199)

Rare and usually linked with now neglected habitation.
Like Canadian Goldenrod but not downy.
Height - 2 metres

Tansy

Tanacetum vulgare (AP 201)

Tall (1 metre). Compact flattish
head of rayless yellow flowers, like
yellow buttons. Strongly scented.
Leaves pinnate with toothed leaflets.
Height - 1 metre

THE DAISY FAMILY Cont'd...

Groundsel

Senecio vulgaris (AP 205)

Heads almost enclosed in black tipped green bracts. Often with seed-heads of small 'Dandelion clocks'. Leaves narrow and deeply toothed.

Very common garden weed. Much branched with yellow flower-heads. *Height - 25 cms*

Heath Groundsel

Senecio sylvaticus (AP 206)

Like Common Groundsel but taller (to 1 metre). Outer flower-heads have rolled back petals. Bracts have purple tips. Leaves narrow and toothed. *Height - 1 metre*

Sticky Groundsel

Senecio viscosus (AP 206)

Stickily hairy. Outer flower-heads have rolled back petals. Bracts are green without dark tips. Leaves pinnate with rounded leaflets. *Height - 50 cms*

THE DAISY FAMILY Cont'd...

Ploughman's-spikenard

Inula conyzae (AP 198)

Tall sometimes branched; stem purple and downy. Flower-heads dull yellow in loose clusters, no outer ray petals.

Leaves long; lower ones broad, upper ones narrow.
Height - 1 metre

Canadian Fleabane

Conyza canadensis (AP 200)

Flower-heads very pale in loose clusters.
Bracts yellowish-green.
Leaves long and narrow and with fringe of hairs. *Height - 1 metre*

Guernsey Fleabane   Conyza sumatrensis (AP 201)

A rare plant, very similar to Canadian Fleabane, except the bracts are grey-green and downy. The lower leaves have hooked hairs.
Height - 1 metre

THE DAISY FAMILY Cont'd...

Trifid Bur-marigold   **Bidens tripartita (AP 208)**

Flower-heads 20 mms across. Flower-heads compact, (like buttons) and upright. Some-times short ray petals are present. Dark bracts. Leaves long, narrow, toothed and with a small lobe on either side near the base. *Height - 60 cms*

Nodding Bur-marigold   **Bidens cernua (AP 208)**

As Trifid
Bur-marigold
but heads
drooping
downwards
and stem hairy.

Height - 60 cms

Yellow flower heads without a central disc.
Each head born singly on an unbranched, or rarely branched stem. Most of leaves are in basal rosette; very few stem leaves.

Dandelion   **Taraxacum species (AP 192)**

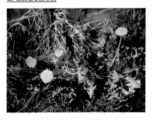

The name 'Dandelion' covers a group of very similar species which are difficult to sepa-rate. For the non-specialist it is enough to lump them all together as 'Dandelions'.
They all have:- Single, hollow leafless stem. Typical flower head followed by 'clock'.
Flower heads 30 mms across. Yellow petals often brown on underside. Toothed leaves in a basal rosette. *Height - 30 cms*

THE DAISY FAMILY Cont'd...

Goat's-beard

Tragopogon pratensis (AP 191)

Flower head like a dandelion but larger (50 mms across) and with fewer petals. Bud is long and drawn out. Leaves almost grass like. Head surrounded by fringe of long thin bracts.

Height - 70 cms

Mouse-ear-hawkweed

Pilosella officinarum (AP 195)

The only one of this group that spreads by runners. Flower heads a lemon-yellow colour. Leaves oval and hairy. Leaf edges curl upwards during dry spells.
Height – 20 cms

Hawkbits

All Hawkbits have tough stems and occasionally the stem branches.

Autumn Hawkbit

Leontodon autumnalis (AP 190)

Most likely to branch a little. Flower head 20 mms across and its base tapers down to the stem. Basal leaves deeply toothed. *Height - 50 cms*

THE DAISY FAMILY Cont'd...

Rough Hawkbit   Leontodon hispidus (AP 190)

Much hairier than Autumn Hawkbit and with few,
if any, branches. Flower head 30 mms across and
only slightly tapering to the top of the stem.
Leaves strongly toothed and hairy.
Height - 60 cms

Lesser Hawkbit   Leontodon saxatilis (AP 190)

Stem with neither leaves nor bracts. Flower head 15 mms across. Leaves and stem
slightly hairy. Leaves in a rosette, bluntly toothed. *Height - 40 cms*

Cat's-ear   Hypochaeris radicata (AP 190)

Stem with small scales and occasionally branching. Flower head 30 mms across.
Bracts seem to be under the flower head rather than enclosing it.
Leaves in rosette narrow and toothed; roughly hairy. *Height - 50 cms*

THE DAISY FAMILY Cont'd...

Smooth Cat's-ear   **Hypochaeris glabra (AP 190)**

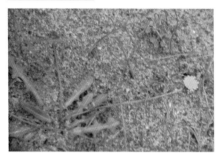

Long slender flower head.
Flowers small (10 mms across) and rarely
opening. Basal rosette leaves long, toothed
and with reddish mid-rib.
Height - 30 cms

Hawkweeds

The *Atlas* records most of the members of this group as very rare or not recorded
recently. Typically they branch near the top of the main stem so that the flowers appear
as a cluster. The flower head is surrounded by several rows of bracts, each covered in
black hairs.

Leaves oval and slightly toothed
(Spotted Hawkweed has marked leaves).
In the flower head, the lower
bracts stand outwards.

Hawk's-beards

Usually well branched and with several rows of bracts surrounding the flower head.

Fox-and-cubs   **Pilosella aurantiaca   (AP 195)**

Cluster of orange-red flower heads. Short stem (30 cms); branches at the top.
Plant has silvery stem covered in thick black hairs. Basal rosette of long narrow leaves;
stem leaves few and of similar shape. *Height - 30 cms*

THE DAISY FAMILY Cont'd…

Rough Hawk's-beard

Crepis biennis (AP 194)

Well branched. Flower heads about 25 mms across. Stem roughly hairy; stem leaves toothed, lobed and without stalk. Basal rosette leaves do have stalks.
Height - 1.2 metres

Smooth Hawk's-beard

Crepis capillaris (AP 194)

Well branched on slender smooth stems. Lower leaves strongly toothed. Upper leaves few, clasp the stem.

Height - 70 cms

Beaked Hawk's-beard

Crepis vesicaria (AP 195)

Well branched. Leaves long, toothed, usually large end-lobe. Leaves divided at the base and often clasping the stem.

Flowers about 20 mms across and orangey-yellow. Stem often reddish and downy; has several rows of bracts and small prickles.

Height - 80 cms

THE DAISY FAMILY Cont'd...

Hawkweed Oxtongue   Picris hieracioides (AP 190)

Flowers about 25 mms across.
Bracts narrow, outer row curving downwards.
Stems reddish and branched.
Leaves toothed and with wavy edges.
Does not have the enlarged bracts of Bristly Oxtongue.
Height - 1 metres

Bristly Oxtongue   Picris echioides (AP 190)

Very bristly, bristles emerge from blister-like swellings. Outer bracts leaf-like and cover the bud. Leaves not toothed. Flowers heads pale yellow, 20 mms across and in loose clusters. *Height - 80 cms*

Nipplewort   Lapsana communis (AP 190)

Flower heads small (15 mms) in much branched clusters.
Leafy branched stem. Lower leaves pinnate with a large toothed end lobe.

Upper leaves toothed, pointed and broadly oval.

Height - 80 cms

THE DAISY FAMILY Cont'd...

Wall Lettuce   Mycelis muralis (AP 192)

A hairless slender plant; exude milky sap if damaged. Leaves pinnate or deeply lobed with large triangular end-lobe. Flowers small (7 mms). *Height - 1.5 metres*

Prickly Lettuce   Lactuca serriola (AP 191)

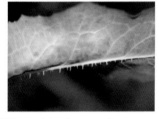

Tall (2 metres). Flowers small (12 mms) in clusters along the stem. Leaves greyish green and with spines/prickles especially on the underside of the mid-rib.
Base of the leaves clasp the stem. *Height - 2 metres*

Sow-thistles
Generally leafier and fleshier members of this Family. They give off a milky sap when damaged.

Perennial Sow-thistle   Sonchus arvensis (AP 191)

Flowers deep yellow. Plant covered in sticky hairs.
Leaves darkish green, slightly toothed and spear shaped.
Height - 1.5 metres

Smooth Sow-thistle   Sonchus oleraceus (AP 191)

 Foliage a grey-green. Flowers pale yellow (about 20 mms across) in clusters. Lower leaves deeply lobed, upper leaves more oval. Base of the leaf forms an arrow-shape on each side of the stem.

Height - 2 metres

Prickly Sow-thistle   Sonchus asper (AP 191)

 Very like Smooth Sow-thistle but deeper yellow flower heads. Base of the leaf is rounded, leaf edge very prickly.
Height - 2 metres

THE BUR-REED FAMILY   SPARGANIACEAE

Despite their name, the Bur-reeds are not closely related to true Reeds. They are aquatic and have strap-shaped leaves which grow up above the water level. The flowers are spherical, without petals and with the male ones above the female ones.

Branched Bur-reed   Sparganium erectum (AP 251)

 The flower spike is branched. When young the male flowers are yellow (pollen) and the female flowers are silvery. Leaves long and and about 12 mms wide, upright. The seed pods are like small conkers.

Height above water - 1 metre

THE BUR-REED FAMILY Cont'd...

Unbranched Bur-reed   **Sparganium emersum (AP 251)**

A rare plant usually found in deeper water than its branched relatives.
The flower spike is unbranched and once the leaves reach the surface they often bend
and float on the water. The seed pods are also like small conkers.

Least Bur-reed   **Sparganium natans (AP 251)**

Very rare. Small, about 25 cms long.
Flower spike usually with one roundish
head, stands about 4 cms above water
surface. Leaves mostly lie flat on
water surface.
Height - 25 cms

THE BULRUSH FAMILY   TYPHACEAE

The two members of this family both have the traditional shape. Both live in shallow water.

Bulrush   **Typha latifolia (AP 252)**

Tall, about 2 metres above the water level.
The lower female part of the flower is
velvety-brown. The upper male part of
the flower is straw-coloured and
immediately above the female part.
Height - 2 metres above the water

THE BULRUSH FAMILY Cont'd…

Lesser Bulrush
Typha angustifolia (AP 252)

Height above water level - 1.5 metres

Smaller, about 1.5 metres above the water surface. There is a gap of about 5 cms between the lower female flowers and the upper male ones.

FLOWERING RUSH FAMILY   BUTOMACEAE

The *Atlas* records only one member of this Family.

Flowering-rush
Butomus umbellatus (AP 209)

This is not a rush, it has a rush-like stem. Flower head is a spray of three- petalled pink flowers. Leaves are grass like. Usually growing in shallow water.
Height - 1.5 metres

WATER-PLANTAIN FAMILY   ALISMATACEAE

The members of this Family all grow in water.

Arrowhead
Sagittaria sagittifolia (AP 209)

Very distinctive green arrowhead leaves appear above water. Flowers in small whorls. Flowers each have 3 white petals each with a purple centre.
Height above water surface - 50 cms

THE WATER PLANTAIN FAMILY Cont'd....

Water-plantain   **Alisma plantago-aquatica (AP 210)**

Tall (1 metre) above water
surface. Pointed oval leaves
appear above water surface.
Flowers in branched whorls.
Each flower with 3 pale
lilac petals.
Height above water - 1 metre

Narrow-leaved Water-plantain   **Alisma lanceolatum (AP 210)**

Similar to Water-plantain but with narrower leaves.
Flowers sometimes pink rather than lilac. *Height above water - 1 metre*

Lesser Water-plantain   **Baldellia ranunculoides (AP 209)**

Short (15 cms) mat forming just under or at the water surface. Leaves narrow-oval.
Seed heads persist and are knobbly, spherical. Flowers pink/white with 3 petals.
Flowers solitary or in very small clusters (2 or 3). *Height above water - 15 cms*

THE WATER PLANTAIN FAMILY Cont'd....

Frogbit

Hydrocharis morsus-ranae (AP 210)

Like small (3 cms) water-lily leaves. Plant is free floating, spreads by runners, soon covers a large area. Small (2 cms) white three petalled flowers on longish stalks.
Height above water - 5 cms

Water-soldier

Stratiotes aloides (AP 210)

Toothed leaves form a spiky rosette. Submerged for much of the year.
Flowers are white with 3 petals. Male flowers in small clusters, female flowers solitary.
Height - 40 cms

Canadian Waterweed (Pondweed)

Elodea canadensis (AP 210)

Leaves in whorls of about three; leaves about 10 cms long. Flowers insignificant. Totally submerged.
In clear water the leaves are closely packed: in murky water they are further apart.
Length - up to 30 cms

Nuttall's Waterweed

Elodea nuttallii (AP 210)

Like Canadian Waterweed but leaves longer (15 cms). Thinner, tapering to a point and turning back along the stem. Leaf whorls very close together. Flowers insignificant.
Length - up to 50 cms

THE WATER PLANTAIN FAMILY Cont'd....

Curly Waterweed   Lagarosiphon major (AP 211)

A rare aquatic introduction. Long, curly and toothed leaves which are arranged in a spiral round the stem. Stem rooted in mud. Inconspicuous flowers.
Length - up to 2 metres

ARROWGRASS FAMILY   JUNCAGINACEAE

Grow near or in water. Long, grass-like leaves. Small, green flowers in spikes.

Sea Arrowgrass   Triglochin maritimum (AP 211)

Flowers in spikes, each flower has a very short stalk. Leaves grass-like. Usually near coast. Flowers with 6 petals/sepals. Style form short white tuft.
Height - 60 cms

Marsh Arrowgrass   Triglochin palustre (AP 211)

Very similar to Sea Arrowgrass, but can occur near any water. Leaves grass-like but furrowed. Seed pod has a longer central, upward pointing section.
Height - 60 cms

THE PONDWEED FAMILY   POTAMOGETONACEAE

All the members of this Family are aquatic, usually living in still or slow moving water. Some are completely submerged, others have floating leaves. The flowers are without petals, but have 4 greenish sepals. The flowers are in short spikes on stems which merge above the water surface. The flowers sink soon after pollination. The leaves vary in shape but apart from Opposite-leaved Pondweed they are all spaced alternately along the stem.

Opposite-leaved Pondweed   Groenlandia densa (AP 213)

The only one with leaves opposite in pairs.
All the leaves (up to 40 mms) are submerged.
Length of leaves - 40 mms

The remaining Pondweeds can be divided into three groups:–
Those with some floating leaves.
Those with broadish leaves but all submerged.
Those with narrow thread-like leaves.

Those with some floating leaves
Broad-leaved Pondweed   Potamogeton natans (AP 211)

Large (120 mm) green oval,
pointed, floating leaves.
Has some submerged leaves.
Length of leaves 80 mms

THE PONDWEED FAMILY Cont'd....

Bog Pondweed   **Potamogeton polygonifolius (AP 211)**

In acid water. Submerged leaves long and narrow. Surface leaves heart-shaped and reddish with obvious veins running length of leaf. *Leaves up to - 100 mms long.*

Fen Pondweed   **Potamogeton coloratus (AP 211)**

Floating leaves are narrow oval in shape and often reddish brown.
Has prominent cross veins linking the long ones. Usually in alkaline water.
Length of leaves - 80 mms

The next three pondweeds have leaves with at least some breadth to them.

All have their leaves submerged.

Curled Pondweed   **Potamogeton crispus (AP 213)**

Leaves slightly toothed
and with very wavy edges.
Stem often reddish
and four angled.
Length of leaves -
40 to 60 mms

Perfoliate Pondweed   **Potamogeton perfoliatus (AP 212)**

A rare pondweed of deeper water. The dark-green, elliptical leaves clasp the stem.
Length of leaves - up to 100 mms

THE PONDWEED FAMILY Cont'd....

Shining Pondweed   Potamogeton lucens (AP 212)

Broad leaves with wavy edges. Leaves translucent with
noticeable veins. Flowers/seed pods look very heavy.
Length of leaves - 6 cms

The remaining four Pondweeds have very narrow leaves.

Small Pondweed   Potamogeton berchtoldii (AP 212)

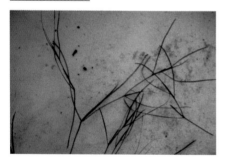

Stem slightly flattened. Leaves with three
veins and air spaces along the mid-rib.
Leaves blunt-tipped and less than 2 mms
wide. In acid water.
Length of leaves - 50 mms

Lesser Pondweed   Potamogeton pusillus (AP 212)

A rare plant. Leaves long, thin about 1.5 mms wide and pointed at the tip.
No air space along the mid rib. Usually in alkaline water.
Length of leaves - 50 mms

THE PONDWEED FAMILY Cont'd....

Hairlike Pondweed   **Potamogeton trichoides (AP 212)**

Very narrow leaves (1 mm) Only one vein running down centre of leaf.
Length of leaves - 50 mms

Fennel Pondweed   **Potamogeton pectinatus (AP 213)**

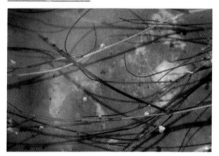
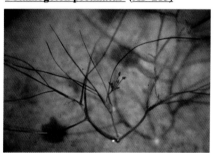

Slightly broader leaves (4 mms). Long sheath below the leaves. Well branched.
Fruit spread along the spike. *Length of leaves up to 1 metre*

THE TASSELWEED FAMILY   **RUPPIACEAE**

Beaked Tasselweed   **Ruppia maritima (AP 213)**

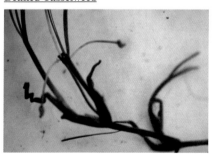
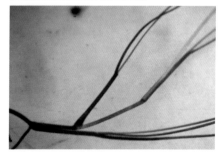

Flowers without petals or sepals. Submerged threadlike leaves (1 mm diameter).
Flowers in clusters of pairs at top of long stalks. In saline or brackish water.
Length - 30 cms

THE HORNED PONDWEED FAMILY

Horned Pondweed

ZANNICHELLIACEAE

Zannichellia palustris (AP 213)

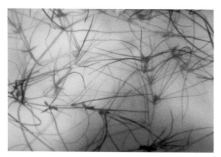

Submerged, thread-like leaves about 1.5 mms wide. *Length - 50 cms*

Flowers stalkless clusters in angle of leaves.

THE ARUM FAMILY

Sweet-flag

ARACEAE

Acorus calamus (AP 214)

Occurs in shallow water. Tall (1 metre).
Long narrow leaves, often with crinkly edges.
Small greenish-yellow flowers in a banana-shaped spike growing out from the upper half of the stem.
Frequently does not flower.
Height - 1 metre

Lords-and-Ladies

Arum maculatum (AP 214)

Arrowhead shaped leaves. Flower is purple spike within a very pale green, (often with purple spots) hood. After the hood has died back, a cluster of red berries develop at the top of the spike.

Height - 30 cms

327

THE ARUM FAMILY Cont'd....

Italian Lords-and-Ladies   Arum italicum (AP 214)

Like the normal form but with the leaves marbled and the hood not spotted.
Berries form and turn red as the flower dies. *Height - 40 cms*

American Skunk-cabbage   Lysichiton americanus (AP 214)

As Lords-and-Ladies but with a green-yellow spike and a bright yellow hood.
Height - 40 cms

THE DUCKWEED FAMILY   LEMNACEAE

Small, free-floating plants in still or slow moving water. Ivy-leaved Duckweed floats
just below the surface, the remainder float on the surface. Flowers, when they occur,
are insignificant.

This photograph shows four species.
The larges ones are greater Duckweed.
The brownish ones with a convex upper
surface are Fat Duckweed. The oval, flat,
green ones are Common Duckweed.
The very small 'pin-head' ones are
Rootless Duckweed.

THE DUCKWEED FAMILY Cont'd....

Ivy-leaved Duckweed

Leaves - 10 mms long

Lemna trisulca (AP 215)

Semi-transparent leaves are a distinctive shape. Leaves float just below the surface. leaflets grow out at right-angles to each other.

Greater Duckweed

Height - 10 mms long

Spirodela polyrhiza (AP 215)

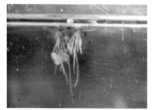

Oval, disc-shaped leaves float on the water surface. Leaves often have a purple tinge, especially on the underside. Has more than one root hanging down into the water.

Fat Duckweed

Leaves - 5 mms across

Lemna gibba (AP 215)

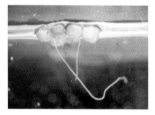

Leaves roughly circular discs which float on water surface. Upper surface is convex and lower surface even more so; appears like a large blister. Has one root hanging into the water.

Rootless Duckweed

Wolffia arrhiza (AP 215)

Leaves very small (1 mm) like green pinheads. Feels gritty if rubbed between fingers. Has no roots. The photograph includes a few leaflets of the "larger" Common Duckweed for size comparison.
Leaves - 1 mm

329

THE DUCKWEED FAMILY Cont'd....

Common Duckweed   Lemna minor (AP 215)

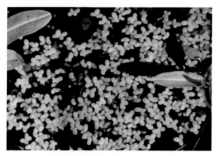 

Round green leaves which float on the surface. Leaves about 4 mms across. Has one root hanging below. *Length of leaves 4 mms*

Least Duckweed   Lemna minuta (AP 215)

Very similar but slightly smaller than Common Duckweed. A fairly recent (1977) arrival in this country; it has now spread rapidly. Round pale-green elliptical leaves which float on the surface. Leaves about 2 mms across. Has one root hanging below. The photograph includes a few fronds of Common Duckweed. *Length of leaves - 2 mms*

Following the sequence of Families as in the *Atlas*, the next ones would be the Rushes, Sedges, etc. these have been transferred to P 351 onwards for the reasons set out there.

THE LILY FAMILY   LILIACEAE

Flowers normally with a total of 6 petals/sepals in two close whorls. Leaves long and thin. Most have bulbs or corms. Distinctive flowers which need little descriptive text.

Bog Asphodel   Narthecium ossifragum (AP 252)

 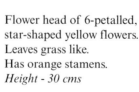 

Flower head of 6-petalled, star-shaped yellow flowers. Leaves grass like. Has orange stamens. *Height - 30 cms*

THE LILY FAMILY Cont'd....

Yellow Day-lily
Hemerocallis lilioasphodelus (AP 252)

Large (7 cms) yellow flowers. Flowers in clusters, each flower short lived.
Leaves long and narrow. *Height - 80 cms*

Meadow Saffron
Colchicum autumnale (AP 253)

Late flowering; flowers after leaves have died back. 6 pink-purple petals, each petal
tapering down to a white stalk. 6 stamens. Leaves long and elliptical.
Height - 25 cms

Wild Tulip
Tulipa sylvestris (AP 253)

Smaller flowers
than typical
Garden Tulip.
Leaves elliptical.
Petals yellow.
Flower stalks
are bent as they
carry buds.

Height - 40 cms

THE LILY FAMILY Cont'd....

Garden Tulip   **Tulipa gesneriana (AP 253)**

Garden escape or relic of old gardens. Flowers solitary. Leaves elliptical.
Range of colours but usually with a black mark at the base of the petals.
Height - 60 cms

Fritillary   **Fritillaria meleagris (AP 253)**

Solitary flowers, drooping and bell-like. Leaves grass-like.
Petals usually purple with darker network of lines; occasionally white petals.
Height - 30 cms

Martagon Lily   **Lilium martagon (AP 253)**

Flowers purple with darker markings. Petals turn back, revealing anthers and style.
Leaves narrow in whorls along the stem. *Height - 1.2 metres*

THE LILY FAMILY Cont'd....

Pyrenean Lily   Lilium pyrenaicum   (AP 253)

Petals yellow
with dark spots.
Petals turn back
revealing
anthers and
style. Long thin
leaves in spiral
along the stem.

Herb Paris   Paris quadrifolia (AP 255)

Flower head just above
four leaves in a cross
arrangement. Flower has
very narrow petals and
sepals around a purple
ovary. A woodland species.
Height - 30 cms

Solomon's-seal   Polygonatum multiflorum (AP 254)

Smooth, arching stem from
which hang creamy-white
bell-shaped flowers. Petals
have green tips. Leaves
broad and pointed,
alternating along the stem.
Height - 80cms

Lily-of-the-valley   Convallaria majalis (AP 254)

White bell-shaped flowers,
in a more or less one
sided spike. Usually two
broadly elliptical leaves.
Red berries.
Height - 25 cms

THE LILY FAMILY Cont'd....

Star-of Bethlehem

Clusters of white 6 petalled star-like flowers. Leaves grass-like.

Ornithogalum angustifolium (AP 255)

Petals have a green stripe down the back.
Height - 25 cms

Spiked Star-of Bethlehem

Ornithogalum pyrenaicum (AP 255)

Also known as Bath Asparagus.
Individual flowers made up of 6 white petals.
Flowers in a spike.
Height - 60 cms

Bluebell

Height - 30 cms

Hyacinthoides non-scripta (AP 255)

Blue hanging bell-shaped flowers, opening to show five lobes. Stem has slight curve so that flowers appear on same side. Leaves long and narrow.

THE LILY FAMILY Cont'd....

Spanish Bluebell

Height - 30 cms

Hyacinthoides hispanica (AP 256)

Hybrids between this and the native Bluebell often appear. Flowers pale blue and stand out all round the stem. Plant is stouter and more upright than the native species.

Glory-of-the-snow

Petals pale lilac or blue with white centre. *Height - 20 cms*

Chionodoxa forbesii (AP 256)

Flower opens to star-shape rather than bell-shape. Leaves long and narrow.

Siberian Squill

Flowers deep blue, petals have darker line down centre of back. Star-shaped but turned downwards.

Scilla siberica (AP 255)

Very small bracts at the base of the petals.
Height - 25 cms

THE LILY FAMILY Cont'd....

Garden Grape-hyacinth

Height - 30 cms

Muscari armeniacum (AP 256)

Closely packed cluster of small blue oval flowers. Opening to the petal 'bulb' is white. Leaves long, narrow and fleshy.

Garlics, Leeks, Onions and Chives are all closely related.

Honey Garlic

Nectaroscordum siculum (AP 258)

Tall (1.2 metres). Flowers are green-brown and hang downwards as they mature. Individual flowers are bell-shaped. Does not have aerial bulbils.
Height - 1.2 metres

Chives

Allium schoenoprasum (AP 257)

Almost globular head of pink-purple flower heads. No bulbils. Two thin bracts. Petals have dark vein down centre. *Height - 25 cms*

THE LILY FAMILY Cont'd....

Rosy Garlic   **Allium roseum (AP 257)**

Pink flowers which spray out from a central point. Sometimes has bulbils. Short bracts.
Height - 25 cms

Keeled Garlic   **Allium carinatum (AP 258)**

Few pink flowers.
Bulbils present.
Long papery
narrow bracts.
Height - 50 cms

Wild Onion (Crow Garlic)   **Allium vineale (AP 258)**

Usually only purple
bulbils are present.
Flowers, if present,
usually pink. Leaves
semi-circular in section.
Broad papery bracts.
Height - 1 metre

Three-cornered Leek   **Allium triquetrum (AP 257)**

Head of white, nodding,
bell–shaped flowers. Stem
sharply triangular in cross
section. Leaves V-shaped
in cross section.
Height - 30 cms

THE LILY FAMILY Cont'd....

Few-flowered Garlic

Usually 3 or 4 white flowers
which hardly open.
Height - 25 cms

Allium paradoxum (AP 257)

Flowers are bulbous at the base and
often the petals close to a point.

Field Garlic

Allium oleraceum (AP 257)

Tall (80 cms). Flower head made up of
bulbils and whitish bell-shaped flowers.
Leaves sheath the ridged stem.
Three long bracts.
Height - 80 cms

Ramsons

Upright stems holding spreading sprays
of white flowers. Broad elliptical leaves.

Allium ursinum (AP 257)

Has very strong 'garlic' smell.
Height - 30 cms

THE LILY FAMILY Cont'd....

Neapolitan Garlic   Allium neapolitanum (AP 257)

 Spray of white flowers arranged like a pin-cushion, opening out to 8 pointed stars. Stem thin and wiry, slightly triangular in section. Leaves V-shaped in section. Bulbils absent.

Height - 30 cms

Hairy Garlic   Allium subhirsutum (AP 257)

Very like Neapolitan Garlic but with rounded, hairy stem.
It is limited to a few verges where its continuity is uncertain.
Height - 30 cms

Snowdrops and Snowflakes

Like all the other members of the Lily Family, the flowers are made of 6 petals/sepals. In Snowflakes, the parts are all alike and form a hanging white bell. In Snowdrops there is a distinct outer ring of 3 white petals and an inner group of 3 arranged somewhat like a tube.

Spring Snowflake   Leucojum vernum (AP 258)

Petals and sepals very much alike and together form a white bell with 6 yellow fringes. Flowers are carried singly or in pairs. Flowers from January onwards.
Height - 30 cms

THE LILY FAMILY Cont'd….

Summer Snowflake

Petals and sepals very much alike and together form a white bell with 6 green fringes.

Leucojum aestivum (AP 258)

Flowers usually in groups of 3 or 4. Despite the name, it flowers in Spring.
Height - 50 cms

Greater Snowdrop

Galanthus elwesii (AP 259)

The largest Snowdrop; outer 'petals' up to 30 mms long. Inner petals strongly marked with green, usually either in shape of a 'X' or an 'H'. Leaves relatively broad.
Height - 30 cms

Caucasian Snowdrop

Galanthus elwesii (Sub species) (AP 259)

Now regarded as a smaller sub species of the Greater Snowdrop. Usually has less green marking on the inner petals.
Height - 15 cms

THE LILY FAMILY Cont'd....

Pleated Snowdrop

Leaves with a fold along their length and a grey-green stripe along the midrib.
Height - 15 cms

Galanthus plicatus (AP 259)

Outer 'petals' about 20 mms long and narrower than other forms. Inner 'petals' have a green tip.

Woronow's Snowdrop

Leaves a rich bright green. As the leaves develop, they are closed at the tip to form a hood.

Galanthus ikariae (AP 259)

Outer 'petals' about 20 mms long. Inner 'petals' have a green patch at the tip.
Height - 15 cms

Snowdrop

Entire upper side of leaf is grey-green.
Height - 20 cms

Galanthus nivalis (AP 258)

Outer 'petals' about 12 mms long. Inner 'petals' green at the tip.

THE LILY FAMILY Cont'd....

Spring Starflower (Ipheion)

Tristagma uniflorum (AP 258)

Garden bulb often naturalised. Has 6 petals/sepals forming a star-shape. Outer part of the flower is violet/blue which fades to white towards the centre. Flowers solitary.
Height - 15 cms

Daffodils

Very familiar as a garden and a cut flower.

Garden Daffodil

Narcissus varieties (AP 260)

The well-known garden flower.
Now frequently planted at the roadside.
Height - 40 cms

Wild Daffodil

Narcissus pseudonarcissus (AP 259)

Smaller than the garden
forms. Trumpet usually
a darker yellow than
the outer ring.
Height - 30 cms

Pheasant's-eye Daffodil

Narcissus poeticus (AP 259)

Outer 'petals' white. Inner 'petals'
orange yellow and much shorter.
Height - 50 cms

THE LILY FAMILY Cont'd….

Garden Asparagus   Asparagus officinalis (AP 260)

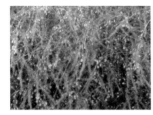  

Very delicate 'filmy' plant. Small (5 mms) creamy yellow flowers. Much branched with finely divided leaves. Fruit is a red berry. *Height - 1.5 metres*

Butcher's-broom   Ruscus aculeatus (AP 260)

Shrub with tough 'leaves' ending in a spike. The leaves are really flattened stems. Pale cream flowers appear to grow out from the middle of the 'leaves'. Fruit a red berry. *Height – 1 metre*

Irises

They can be distinguished by their arrangement of the 3 inner and the 3 outer 'petals'. The outer 3 bend outwards and downwards and are called 'the falls'. The individual species can be distinguished by their colour.

Yellow Iris (Flag)   Iris pseudacorus (AP 261)

Bright yellow flowers. Sword-like leaves. Usually near water. *Height – 1 metre*

THE LILY FAMILY Cont'd....

Snake's-head Iris   Hermodactylus tuberosus (AP 260)

Flowers with inner 'petals' yellowy-
green and outer ones purple.
Leaves thin and almost square in section.
Height - 30 cms

Stinking Iris   Iris foetidissima (AP 261)

Flowers pale lilac and light-brown. Veins
clearly marked. Leaves sword-shaped;
when crushed have distinct smell.
Height - 60 cms

Some say it smells like roast beef, others
disagree. Has three seed pods with
bright red seeds.

Bearded Iris   Iris germanica (AP 261)

The large garden form. Has yellow hairs
in the centre of each fall, (the 'beard').
Height - 1 metre

Has large swollen root-like stem
rhizomes at ground level.

THE LILY FAMILY Cont'd....

Crocuses

6 petals/sepals surrounding 3 short stamens and a feathery orange stigma.

Early Crocus   **Crocus tommasinianus (AP 261)**

Slender flowers. Flowers pale blue shading to white at the base. Leaves very narrow.
Height - 25 cms

Eastern Gladiolus   **Gladiolus communis (AP 262)**

A garden escape. Flower stems sometimes branched. Flowers magenta, usually more
than 10 in a spike. *Height - 1 metre*

Aunt-Eliza   **Crocosmia paniculata (AP 262)**

Form of the common Montbretia. Flowers orange-red. Petal lobes about half the length
of the petal tube. Leaves sword shaped and pleated. *Height - 1.2 metres*

THE LILY FAMILY Cont'd....

Montbretia   Crocosmia x crocosmiiflora (AP 262)

A garden hybrid now well established in the wild. Clump forming. Flowers orange/red. Petal lobes about the same length as the petal tube. Leaves spear-shaped but not pleated.
Height - 70 cms

THE YAM FAMILY   DIOSCOREACEAE

Black Bryony   Tamus communis (AP 263)

On first sight very unlike the Lilies. Sprawling climber. Side branches carry spikes of pale-green, 6 petalled male flowers. Female flowers are in tighter clusters. Leaves are heart-shaped. Fruit a cluster of red berries.
Height - scrambling to 3 metres

THE ORCHID FAMILY   ORCHIDACEAE

The British orchids grow from the ground. Flowers are in unbranched spikes. The flower is made up of three sepals, usually coloured, and three petals, one forming a lip. There is a single bract at the base of each flower. Helleborines should not be confused with hellebores.

White Helleborine   Cephalanthera damasonium (AP 263)

Creamy-white flowers which often remain unopened. Base of the lip is orange-yellow. Leaves are elliptical and cover much of the stem.
Height - 50 cms

THE ORCHID FAMILY Cont'd....

Broad-leaved Helleborine   Epipactis helleborine (AP 263)

Flowers greeny-yellow with a
purple tinge. Lip petal is darker
red/purple. Has longish bracts.
Middle leaves are broad ellipse,
ones above and below are
narrower.
Height - 70 cms

Marsh Helleborine   Epipactis palustris (AP 263)

Flowers in shades of cream and
brown. Lower lip petal has white
frill against a cream background.
Grows in marshy areas,
especially dune slacks.
Height - 30 cms

Bird's-nest Orchid   Neottia nidus-avis (AP 263)

Without chlorophyll. Stem is pale brown. Flower is also brown, outer petals fold over to
give the flower a spherical look. The lower petal is markedly forked. *Height - 40 cms*

Autumn Lady's-tresses   <u>Spiranthes spiralis</u> (<u>AP 264</u>)

Small white flowers spiralling
up the stem. Flowers only
open at the tip.
Oval base leaves soon wither;
stem leaves are scale-like.
Height - 15 cms

Common Twayblade   <u>Listera ovata</u> (<u>AP 264</u>)

Distinct pair of oval leaves
("blades") with stem emerging
from between them.
Flowers yellow-green with
long, forked, hanging lip petal.
Height - 40 cms

Greater Butterfly-orchid   <u>Platanthera chlorantha</u> (<u>AP 264</u>)

Flower creamy-white. Long lip at the front and a spur at the
back. Inside the 'throat' the yellow pollen sacs diverge and
spread outwards. Base leaves elliptical, stem leaves small.
Often on the edge of hillside woods.
Height - 40 cms

Lesser Butterfly-orchid   **Platanthera bifolia (AP 264)**

Like the Greater form but smaller and has strong scent. The pollen sacs in the 'throat' lie parallel to each other. Usually grows in marshy ground.
Height - 30 cms

Lizard Orchid   **Himantoglossum hircinum (AP 267)**

Height - 60 cms

Large green-brown flowers. Very long (40 mms) twisted tongue, (lip petal). Short spur. Associated with light sandy soils on the Burnham/ Berrow dunes.

THE ORCHID FAMILY Cont'd....

Bee Orchid

Ophrys apifera (AP 267)

Large lobed lip
looking bee-like.
Surrounded by
3 pink sepals.

Height - 30 cms

Fly Orchid

Ophrys insectifera (AP 267)

Lip part of flower dark brown with a
blue 'waist' which turns yellow when the
flower is pollinated.

Outer sepals cream.
Height - 30 cms

Frog Orchid

Coeloglossum viride (AP 265)

Flowers yellow-green with
brown markings.
Said to resemble side view
of a jumping frog.
Lip petal short and forked
with a tongue in the centre.
Height - 15 cms

THE ORCHID FAMILY Cont'd....

Pyramidal Orchid   **Anacamptis pyramidalis (AP 265)**

Petals a vibrant pink. Flower head   Lip petal broad and deeply lobed.
appears as short cone of flowers.   *Height - 30 cms*

Green-winged Orchid   **Orchis morio (AP 266)**

Flower ranges from white (rarely) to   Outer petals show green veins.
shades of purple. Has dark markings on The smallest of the 'purple' orchids.
inner petals.   *Height - 15 cms*

Fragrant Orchid   **Gymnadenia conopsea (AP 265)**

Flowers pink/purple.
Very long spur. Scented.
Height - 30 cms

Early-purple Orchid   Orchis mascula (AP 266)

Flowers a strong purple
colour. At maturity the
sepals (outer wing petals)
fold up and over to
touch each other.
The lip petal is broad
with a short tongue.
Leaves strongly spotted.
Height - 30 cms

Common Spotted-orchid   Dactylorhiza fuchsii (AP 265)

Flowers produced in long, dense spikes. Colour varies from pale to dark red-purple.
The lip petal has dark markings, usually in form of lines. The tongue in the centre of the
lip petal is pointed and protrudes. Stem is firm and solid.
Height - 40 cms

THE ORCHID FAMILY Cont'd....

Heath Spotted-orchid   Dactylorhiza maculata (AP 265)

Flowers in short head.
Stem is firm and solid.
Leaves usually spotted.
Colour varies from white
to pink-purple. Lip petal
has streaks and spots.
The tongue in the centre
does not protrude.
Height - 30 cms

Early Marsh-orchid   Dactylorhiza incarnata (AP 266)

Flowers are usually pink/purple with dark
lines. Sides of lip petal soon fold back to
make the flower appear narrow and spiky.
Stems feel very hollow. Leaves pale green
and usually without spots.
Height - 20 cms

Flowers are sometimes a
salmon pink colour.

THE ORCHID FAMILY Cont'd....

Southern Marsh-orchid   **Dactylorhiza praetermissa (AP 266)**

Tall (60 cms). Flowers range
from pale pink to purple.
Lip petal is broader than long.
Tongue is short and blunt.
Centre of lip is usually pale
with darker dots and streaks.
Stem hollow. Lower leaves
usually without spots.
Height - 60 cms

RUSHES, SEDGES, GRASSES AND SIMILAR FAMILIES

As explained on Page 327 we have transferred these Families to the end of the book.
To identify individual species involves absorbing extra botanical terms, something few
people, with a general interest in plants, want to undertake. As in the rest of the book, we
have tried to avoid "technical" terms but to do this, we have limited ourselves to the briefest
accounts of how to differentiate between the Families. We feel that many users of this
guide will be pleased if they can distinguish between say a Wood-rush and a Sedge.

For those wanting to go a bit further, we have picked out those species most likely to
be seen and given a brief description of them.

For any reader who does want more detail, we suggest reference to:-

*Colour identification Guide to the Grasses, Sedges, Rushes and Ferns of the British Isles and
north-western Europe*, by Francis Rose published by Viking (Penguin Group), London
1989. Or *Grasses, Sedges Rushes and Ferns* published by Collins Guide, London 1984.
Or *Grasses* by C E Hubbard published by Penguin (Reprint) 1992.

RUSHES   JUNCACEAE

Usually erect, tussocky plants growing in marshy habitats. Stems are hairless and cylindrical. Leaves are long, slender and sheath the stem. Flowers are small green/brown and
with 6 very small petals or sepals. The flowers are usually in tufted clusters either at the
top of the stem or at the side. The *Atlas* identifies 17 species (excluding hybrids).

THE RUSH FAMILY Cont'd....

Compact Rush

Tall. Flowers in tight clusters at side of stem.
Height - 80 cms

Juncus conglomeratus (AP 218)

Soft-rush

Tall. Flowers in loose clusters at side of stem. Stem fattish, bright green and can easily be squeezed between the fingers. This is the species which gave the wick for a "rush light".

Juncus effusus (AP 218)

Height - 60 cms

Hard Rush

Juncus inflexus (AP 218)

Tall. Flowers in a small loose cluster at side of stem. Stem hard, bluish-green and ridged.
Height - 60 cms

Jointed Rush   Juncus articulatus (AP 217)

Tall. Flowers in loose clusters near the top of stem. Transverse 'joints' can be felt at intervals along the stem.
Height - 60 cms

Sharp-flowered Rush   Juncus acutiflorus (AP 217)

Tall. Sharply pointed flowers in loose spray at top of stem.

Height - 80 cms

Bulbous Rush   Juncus bulbosus (AP 218)

Low growing. Flowers red-brown and spaced along the stem. Leaves bright-green and with bulb-like swelling at the base.

Height - 20 cms

Toad Rush   Juncus bufonius (AP 217)

Low growing. Stem branching to form a mini bush. Flowers in fork of branches and spaced along the stem.
Height - 29 cms

WOODRUSHES   LUZULA

Usually with hairy, limp and flat grass-like leaves. Flowers small yellow or brown in loose clusters at top of the stem. The *Atlas* identifies 6 species.

Field Wood-rush   Luzula campestris (AP 219)

A compact cluster of brown heads each with conspicuous yellow anthers. Leaves hairy and grass like. *Height - 15 cms*

Heath Wood-rush   Luzula multiflora (AP 219)

Numerous flowers on stalks of different lengths in a fairly compact head. *Height - 30 cms*

Hairy Wood-rush   Luzula pilosa (AP 219)

Glossy bright-green leaves, densely hairy. Flower brown on radiating stalks of different lengths. As flowers develop they open out into a loose cluster. *Height - 25 cms*

COTTON GRASS   ERIOPHORUM

Grass-like plants with flower heads like tufts of cotton wool. Usually growing in boggy ground. The *Atlas* identifies three species still present.

Common Cottongrass   **Eriophorum angustifolium (AP 219)**

Flower-head of several clusters of flowers each carrying silky white threads.
Height - 50 cms

Hare's-tail Cottongrass   **Eriophorum vaginatum (AP 220)**

Flower-head consists
of single head with
silky white threads.
Height - 25 cms

Broad-leaved Cottongrass   **Eriophorum latifolium (AP 220)**

This extremely rare species was only identified from 2 sites, both threatened.
It does have broader leaves. *Height - 25 cms*

Deergrass   **Trichophorum Cespitosum (AP 220)**

Only one species. Forms a tuft of stems with a flower at the tip. Leaves reduced to small scales, which sheath the stem. The topmost scale has a short spike-like blade. This distinguishes Deergrass from the Spike-rushes. *Height - 25 cms*

THE SPIKE RUSH FAMILY

SPIKE-RUSH   ELEOCHARIS

Small rush-like plants with upright stems. Leaves reduced to a sheath at the base of the stem. Flowers like small brown cones at the top of the stem. The *Atlas* refers to 4 species, only one is described as common.

Common Spike-rush   **Eleocharis palustris (AP 220)**

Hairless stems with leaves reduced to short sheaths near the base. Flowers in short spikelets at the top of the stem. Grows near water. *Height - 30 cms*

CLUB-RUSHES   SEVERAL GENERA

Leafless green stems. Flowers at the tip of the true stem but over-topped by a bract which looks like an extension of the stem. The *Atlas* refers to 8 species but regards only two of them as common.

Sea Club-rush   **Bolboschoenus maritimus (AP 221)**

Not confined to the coast. Stems are triangular in section. Flowerhead a compact mass of spikelets which are over-topped by a long, narrow bract. *Height - 60 cms*

Bristle Club-rush   **Isolepis setacea (AP 221)**

Very grass-like with outer sheathing leaves. Flower-head of two to three spikelets. Spike usually extends beyond the flower head. *Height - 20 cms*

FEN-SEDGE

CLADIUM

There is only one species recorded.

Great Fen-sedge

Height - 2 metres

Cladium mariscus (AP 222)

Very tall (2 metres). Leaves V-shaped in section and with fine saw-like edge. Long flowering spike with clusters of fawn/brown flowers along the stem.

SEDGE FAMILY

Carex

Unbranched or rarely branched, usually hairless. Stem is usually triangular in section and leaves are V-shaped in section. Male and female flowers distinct and often in separate spikelets. Usually occur in wet/marshy habitats. The *Atlas* refers to 44 species (with the usual exceptions). About 20 species are common or widespread.

The tall group i.e. usually 1 metre or more in height.

Great Tussock-sedge

Carex paniculata (AP 223)

Forms very large (1 metre across and 1 metre high tussocks). Very often grows in water, (in this picture the water had iced over, allowing the student to stand on it). New growth appears on top of tussock of old material. *Height - 1 metre plus*

THE SEDGE FAMILY Cont'd....

Pendulous Sedge

Very tall stems which droop outwards and downwards. *Height - 2 metres*

Carex pendula (AP 226)

Flowers hang downwards like long thin catkins. Dull brownish green.

Cyperus Sedge

Carex pseudocyperus (AP 225)

Also puts out long stems which then droop downwards. Flowers like fat catkins. Greener than Pendulous Sedge. *Height - 1 metre*

Greater Pond-sedge

Height - 1 metre plus

Carex riparia (AP 225)

Very common on ditch banks. Stem sharply triangular in section and leaves V-shaped in section. Has black feathery male flowers above silvery/gold female ones.

THE SEDGE FAMILY Cont'd....

Bottle Sedge   Carex rostrata (AP 225)

Stem bluntly triangular in section.
Male flowers brown and slim
cigar-shaped, female flowers much fatter.
Height - 1 metre

False Fox-sedge   Carex otrubae (AP 223)

Stem 3 sided.
Flowers green/brown
in thick-shaped dense
spikes. Long bract(s)
at the base of the flower.
Height - 1 metre

Spiked Sedge   Carex spicata (AP 223)

Leaves long and pointed.
Fruits pointed and
often dark red.
Height - 1 metre

THE SEDGE FAMILY Cont'd….

Carnation Sedge

Carex panicea (AP 226)

Grey-green, almost silvery leaves. Only one male catkin.
Height - 30 cms

Glaucous Sedge

Height - 30 cms

Carex flacca (AP 226)

Grey-green
leaves. 2 or 3
male brown
catkins.

Star Sedge

Carex echinata (AP 224)

Few flowers separated into star-shaped clusters.
Similar to Spiked Sedge but smaller. *Height - 20 cms*

THE SEDGE FAMILY Cont'd....

Flea Sedge

Carex pulicaris (AP 229)

Few flowers which are
separated along the stem.
Flowers turn down when ripe.
Height - 20 cms

Pill Sedge

Carex pilulifera (AP 228)

Very short
horizontal
stems which
turn up to give
tussocks. One
central male
flower above
about 3 female
ones. Stem
bends over as
fruit ripens.

Height - 30 cms

Spring-sedge

Carex caryophyllea (AP 228)

Leaves dark green. Short stiff stem with
red-brown female flowers. Lower bract just
over half as long as the flower spike.
Height - 30 cms

THE SEDGE FAMILY Cont'd....

Medium-sized Sedges (40 to 60 cms tall)

All have three-sided stems.

Wood-sedge

Slender stem arching upwards and outwards from a tussock. *Height - 50 cms*

Carex sylvatica (AP 226)

Typically in woodland.
Long slender flower spikes.

Oval Sedge

Height - 50 cms

Carex ovalis (AP 224)

Largish oval/round flower spikes, clustered at the top of the stem.

Remote Sedge

Slender pale-green leaves.
Height - 40 cms

Carex remota (AP 224)

Small flower spikes well spaced out along the stem.

THE SEDGE FAMILY Cont'd....

Grey Sedge

Carex divulsa (AP 223)

Loose and spikey flower-heads scattered along the stem. *Height - 40 cms*

Common Sedge

Carex nigra (AP 229)

Male flowers are small black spikes. Female flowers are sausage-shaped, green with black 'outer scales'.

Height - 60 cms

Common Yellow-sedge

Carex viridula (AP 228)

Pale yellow-green leaves. Fawn male spike at the top of the stem. 2 or 3 rounded female spikes immediately below the male spike and an odd female spike lower down the stem. *Height - 40 cms*

366

GRASSES

We think that many of the users of this book will be quite content to distinguish grasses from, say, sedges. However, for those who want to go into more detail, we have tried to

indicate how, within the grasses, one can distinguish between e.g. a fescue and a foxtail. For those who want to go even further we have identified some 40 plus individual species which are common and/or widespread and given a brief description of each.

General features of Grasses

Stem round in section. Long thin leaves alternate along opposite side of the stem.

The flowers are petal-less (they are pollinated by wind, not insects) and many are feathery, or rather like small worn-out feather dusters. Some, however, have more distinct features and these have been described first.

Cock's-foot   **Dactylis glomerata (AP 234)**

Stout stem with side branches which carry some 4 or 5 oval clusters of spikelets.

Height - 60 cms

Wood Millet   **Milium effusum (AP 230)**

A tall but light feathery plant, usually in woodland shade. Side branches leave the main stem in groups of 4. They further branch and carry small spikelets. *Height - 1.2 metres*

Several other grasses are called Millets but they are rare casuals and not closely related.

THE GRASS FAMILY Cont'd….

Quaking-grass

Briza media (AP 233)

Slender stem with side
branches carrying pendant,
almost heart-shaped spikelets.
Height - 40 cms

The *Atlas* also records, as a rarity, Greater Quaking-grass.

Crested Dog's-tail

Cynosurus cristatus (AP 232)

The central stem
carries short
spikelets.
The spikelets,
close to the stem,
are arranged
alternately.

Height - 40 cms

Wood Melick

Melica uniflora (AP 236)

Leafy green
with slender
stems. Stems
carry side
branches.
These bear
spikelets either
singly or in
pairs along
their stems.

Height - 40 cms

THE GRASS FAMILY Cont'd....

Fern-grass   Catapodium rigidum (AP 235)

Short stiff stems with short-stalked stiff spikelets. Spikelets either single or in pairs.

Height - 40 cms

The *Atlas* also records Sea Fern-grass as present but rare.

Sweet Vernal Grass   Anthoxanthum odoratum (AP 239)

Strong smell of hay when crushed. Typically found in meadows.

Flower head is a loose spike.
Height - 30 cms

Common Couch   Elytrigia repens (AP 246)

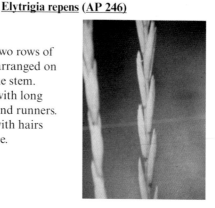

Spike made up of two rows of flattened spikelets arranged on opposite sides of the stem. Often in tufts and with long creeping underground runners. Leaves dull-green with hairs on the upper surface.
Height - 50 cms

THE GRASS FAMILY Cont'd....

Purple Moor-grass   Molinia caerulea (AP 249)

Height - 80 cms

Leaves greyish-green and easily form tussocks. Flower heads purplish when young. Flower heads remain close to the stem and form a narrow spike. The dominant grass on damp peaty soils.

The next 3 grasses all grow at the water's edge. They are quite tall.

Common Reed   Phragmites australis (AP 249)

Leaves often pushed by wind to appear like horizontal rungs of a ladder. Young flower heads a coppery colour. Often forms extensive beds or grows in ranks along a waterway.
Height - 2.5 metres

Reed Canary-grass   Phalaris arundinacea (AP 239)

Clump forming. Leaves broad and rough edged. Head made up of clusters of spikelets on relatively short branches.
Height - 2 metres

THE GRASS FAMILY Cont'd....

Reed Sweet-grass   **Glyceria maxima (AP 235)**

Flower head of loose green
spikelets. Clump forming.
Often grows in the water
(not just on the bank).
Height - 2 metres

Rye-grasses

Flower head consists of spikelets growing close to the stem, giving a 'flat' appearance.
Spikelets alternate along the stem.

Perennial Rye-grass   **Lolium perenne (AP 231)**

Flower heads
without spikes.

Height - 30 cms

Italian Rye-grass   **Lolium multiflorum (AP 232)**

Very like Perennial Rye grass but
flower heads have longish spikes.
Height - 40 cms

THE GRASS FAMILY Cont'd....

Sweet-grasses

Grow in or near water. Flower heads form cigar-shaped groups.

Floating Sweet-grass

Usually in shallow water with some leaves floating flat on the surface. Leaves pale green.

Glyceria fluitans (AP 235)

Flower heads little branched.
Height - 1 metre

Plicate Sweet-grass

Glyceria notata (AP 236)

Leaves dark-green.
Flower heads well branched.
Height - 70 cms

Barleys

A number are escapes from cultivation. Flower made up of a compact cluster of spikelets on an upright stem. Each spikelet has long bristles.

Wall Barley

Height - 25 cms

Hordeum murinum (AP 247)

Tufted growth form. Bristles almost parallel to the main stem.

THE GRASS FAMILY Cont'd....

Meadow Barley   **Hordeum secalinum (AP 248)**

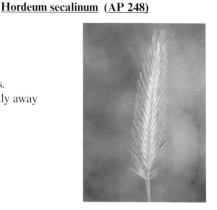

Does not form tufts.
Bristles stand slightly away
from the stem.
Height - 40 cms

Bromes

Another group whose spikelets have long bristles. Unlike the Barleys, the spikelets are
loose and usually drooping.

Soft-brome   **Bromus hordeaceus (AP 244)**

Spikelets on
shortish stalks
and 'fat' looking
rather than
feathery.
Tendency of
flower head to
droop to one
side. Softly
downy.

Height - 60 cms

Hairy Brome   **Bromopsis ramosa (AP 244)**

Tall (1 metre plus). Flower heads on long
drooping stalks.

Heads small. Long bristles.
Height - 1 metre

373

THE GRASS FAMILY Cont'd....

Barren Brome   Anisantha sterilis (AP 245)

Has very long (3 cms or more) bristles.
Medium height (70 cms).
Bristles tend to fan out slightly.
Height - 70 cms

False Brome   Brachypodium sylvaticum (AP 246)

Broad leaves,
slender flower
heads. Bristles
close together.

Height - 50 cms

Oat-grasses

Similar to Bromes. Spikelets have long bristles which are bent in Wild Oat and Yellow Oat-grass.

False Oat-grass   Arrhenatherum elatius (AP 237)

Fattish spikelets with long straight bristles. Shiny.
Height - 1.5 metres

THE GRASS FAMILY Cont'd….

Wild-oat

Avena fatua (AP 237)

Whorls of about 5 branches spreading outwards. *Height - 1 metre*

Spikelets with 2 flowers.
Long bent bristles.

Yellow Oat-grass

Grows in small tufts. Whorls of about 3 side branches, about 4 spikelets per branch.
Flower head upright.
Pale green leaves.

Trisetum flavescens (AP 237)

Height - 60 cms

Foxtails

Have a cluster of one-flowered spikelets arranged to give a 'bulrush' effect.

Meadow Foxtail

Alopecurus pratensis (AP 242)

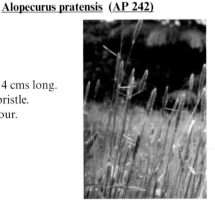

Flower head about 4 cms long.
Each flower has a bristle.
Greyish-purple colour.
Height - 80 cms

THE GRASS FAMILY Cont'd….

Marsh Foxtail   Alopecurus geniculatus   (AP 242)

Creeping growth,
bright-green leaves.
Flower head short and
often purple. Lower
stem joints are knobbly.
Height - 40 cms

Black-grass   Alopecurus myosuroides   (AP 243)

A more tapering
flower head.
Height - 70 cms

Timothy   Phleum pratense   (AP 243)

Very long
(12 cms) flower
head. Flower
head not
tapered.

Height - 1 metre

The Feathery grasses
Soft-grasses

Softly downy. Flower heads often pinkish.

Yorkshire-fog   Holcus lanatus   (AP 238)

Often covers large areas
with mist-like (rather
than fog-like) pinkish-white
haze. Spikelets with two
flowers, each flower has
very short, non-protruding
bristles. *Height - 90 cms*

THE GRASS FAMILY Cont'd....

Creeping Soft-grass

Holcus mollis (AP 239)

Less stocky than Yorkshire Fog and with hairless stem, but stem joints have hairs. Far creeping root stock.

Height - 70 cms

Hair-grasses

Flowers in delicate whorls of four. Two flowers per spikelet. Leaves with ridges and furrows.

Tufted Hair-grass

Deschampsia cespitosa (AP 238)

Tall (to 1 metre). Forms tufts.
Height - 1 metre

Wavy Hair-grass

Deschampsia flexuosa (AP 238)

Short (30 cms). Forms tufts. Flower heads branched and spreading, branches wavy. Each flower has short bristles. *Height - 30 cms*

THE GRASS FAMILY Cont'd....

Bents

Whorls of delicate branches. Whorls in fours. Spikelets have 1 flower.

Common Bent

Height - 80 cms

Agrostis capillaris (AP 240)

Creeping, non leafy, below ground stem. The leaves all arise from the base. Flowers well separated.

Creeping Bent

Height - 60 cms

Agrostis stolonifera (AP 240)

Creeping runners, leafy and rooting and above ground level. Flowers close together.

THE GRASS FAMILY Cont'd....

Meadow-grasses

Flower heads in whorls. Usually 3 or 4 flowers at the end of the branch.
Often have a horizontal stem either on the ground or below it.

Annual Meadow-grass   **Poa annua (AP 233)**

Forms small
tufts. Flower
heads roughly
triangular
in outline.
Spikelets pale
white/green.
3 to 5 flowers
per spikelet.

Height - 15 cms

Rough Meadow-grass   **Poa trivialis (AP 233)**

Spreads by runners, at or just below ground level.
4 to 6 spikelets per branch.
Leaf sheaths very rough.
Height - 40 cms

Smooth Meadow-grass   **Poa pratensis (AP 234)**

Hairless but stiff,
stocky growth.
Flower heads
long narrow
triangular shape.
5 or 6 spikelets
per branch.
Creeping under-
ground stem.

Height - 30 cms

THE GRASS FAMILY Cont'd....

Wood Meadow-grass   Poa nemoralis (AP 234)

Slender, pale whitish-green, much branched flower head. Leaves narrow.
Underground creeping stem. *Height - 50 cms*

Fescues

Side branches singly or in pairs, not whorls. Spikelets in 4s or 5s. Spikelets have bristles.

Meadow Fescue   Festuca pratensis (AP 230)

Spikelets ending in a point
rather than a bristle.
Forms small tufts. Hairless
but leaves have a rough edge.
Flower heads often nodding.
Leaves broad.
Height - 1 metre

Tall Fescue   Festuca arundinacea (AP 230)

Tall (1 metre
plus). Spikelets
usually with
short bristles.
Leaves broad.

Height - 1 metre

THE GRASS FAMILY Cont'd....

Giant Fescue

Festuca gigantea (AP 230)

Tall (1 metre plus). Flower heads with long bristles and drooping to one side. Leaves broad and rough when rubbed downwards. *Height - 1.5 metres*

Red Fescue

Festuca rubra (AP 231)

Height - 30 cms

Forms tufts and has both above and below-ground runners. Small slender flower head. Usually slightly hairy. Spikelets sometimes red but commonly green with a short bristle.

Sheep's Fescue

Festuca ovina (AP 231)

Usually hairless, tufted but not creeping. Thin stem and very narrow leaves. Flower head compact, flowers with a short bristle. Narrow grey-green leaves. Flowers ripen to a dark brown-purple and have a short bristle. *Height - 25 cms*

Index